Contents

Introduction

Wales was a wonderfully wicked country in the olden days. But its history can be HIDEOUSLY boring – especially when your teachers go on . . . and on . . . and on . . . and on about kings and queens and important people who lived in grand houses, wore fashionable clothes (well, they *thought* they were the height of fashion!) and told everyone else what to do.

And when tiresome teachers ask seriously stupid questions, no wonder they get some stunningly silly answers!

FORTUNATELY: by the time of the Troublesome Tudors and the Sleazy Stuarts – in the EARLY MODERN PERIOD – there weren't any kings or queens left in Wales.

UNFORTUNATELY: the kings and queens of **England** now ruled **Wales** too, and lots of Welsh people wanted to go to live with them – in London.

You would think that Wales had disappeared off the map of the British Isles.

Did this mean the end of Welsh history? No, worse luck! There were still plenty of important people around and lots and lots of odious ordinary folk (like you and me). No, we can't avoid the hideous history of Wales in the Early Modern Period after all.

An Englishman called Caxton described the ordinary Welsh people (men, of course) who lived at the beginning of the troublesome Tudor Age:

They dress well – a shirt, a cloak and nice trousers – but they never wear anything on their legs.

They can go without food for a long time.

They like to eat barley bread, oatcakes and gruel (a very watery thin porridge – ych-a-fi!).

They drink mead and beer – often all day and all night.

They carry a purse and a comb hanging from their trousers.

They are very fussy – they don't like people who fart (who does?), but they think nothing of peeing just outside their own front door.

(I wonder whether Caxton had ever visited Wales?)

Would you like to know more about these weird and wacky Welsh people?

Then read on – if you want to know the truth about wicked Wales.

A Quaint Quiz about the Early Modern Period – for Starters

1. When was the Early Modern Period?

   (a) After the Old-fashioned Period.
   (b) Before seven o'clock in the morning.
   (c) Between 1485 and 1688.

2. How much Welsh blood did Henry VIII have?

   (a) Not a drip.
   (b) Ten drops.
   (c) A pint.

I do have a drop of Welsh blood in me – honestly!

3. Why did Mary Tudor hate the Protestants?

   (a) Because they protested all the time.
   (b) Because her sister, Elizabeth, was one of them.
   (c) Because she hated everyone, anyway.

4. Why were the Stuarts always in a stew?

   (a) Because they had plenty of leeks and carrots (to make a nice casserole).
   (b) Because King Charles I kept falling out with Parliament.
   (c) Because there wasn't any curry in Stuart times.

5. Who were Queen Mary and Prince William of Orange?

   (a) A queen (and her husband) who ate a lot of oranges.
   (b) A queen (and her husband) who sunbathed all the time and who had orange-coloured skin.
   (c) A queen (and her husband) who came over from Orange in the Netherlands to rule England, Scotland and Wales after 1688.

You don't know the answers? (Tut, tut!)
Why not ask your history teachers? Unfortunately, they probably won't know the answers either. But if you read this hideous history you will, hopefully, know more than they do.

Answers
1(c), 2(c),
3(a+b), 4(b),
5(c).

Getting to know the troublesome Tudors and the sleazy Stuarts

Although this is a book about wicked Wales, it's important to know something about the troublesome Tudor and the sleazy Stuart kings and queens who ruled not only Wales, but also England, and Scotland (after 1603) in the EARLY MODERN PERIOD.

This is their tyrannical timeline:

THE TROUBLESOME TUDORS

What happened in England?	And what about Wales?
HENRY VII – HENRY TUDOR (1485–1509) The first of the troublesome Tudors. He was one quarter Welsh, one quarter French and one half English. He defeated Richard III at the Battle of Bosworth in 1485 and became king of England and Wales. By being a miser he became rich and made his kingdom strong.	Many Welsh people doted on Henry Tudor. His grandfather came from Anglesey, so they thought that, at last, they had a Welshman on the throne of England, and that he would pay wicked Wales a lot of attention. (What do you think?)
HENRY VIII (1509–1547) A strong and cruel king. He wanted to make sure he had a son to rule after him. So he had six wives: he beheaded two of them, divorced two, one died, and the last was alive when Henry died (what luck!).	According to the story, when he was dying, Henry VII asked his son, Henry junior, to look after little Wales (which suggests, of course, that Henry VII hadn't done anything for Wales himself).

THE TROUBLESOME TUDORS

What happened in England?

Because Henry wanted to divorce his first wife, he got rid of the Catholic Church and its Boss – the Pope in Rome – and made himself the Boss of the new Church of England (note – not the Church in Wales!).
He spent his father's fortune.

And what about Wales?

And Henry did do something for Wales – in his own miserable little way – because he united Wales and England through the Acts of Union in 1536–43. (And the people of Wales have been arguing about this ever since.)

I wonder what will happen to me?

VI

EDWARD VI (1547–1553)

Edward was a weak little boy when he became king and, so, a Council had to rule instead of him. Now the Protestants were in power – and the old Catholic customs were forbidden. Every member of the Church of England had to worship in English.

Edward died when he was only sixteen years old. (Poor thing!)

Some Catholics in Wales were sad to see the old traditions being destroyed and English used in the churches instead of Latin. (Though they didn't understand either language, English or Latin!)

Some wanted the church services in Welsh.

THE TROUBLESOME TUDORS

What happened in England?

MARY I (BLOODY MARY) (1553–1558)

She was a Catholic and had married Philip, the Catholic King of Spain. More than 280 Protestants were burned at the stake when Mary Tudor was queen. (Perhaps she should be called Blazing Mary, not Bloody Mary).

ELIZABETH I (1558–1603)

England's Golden Age. Queen Elizabeth had red hair and a fiery temper. She had several lovers (so they say) but she never married. She said she was married to England. (Wasn't that lucky for Wales?) She was a Protestant and there were several plots to get rid of her. The worst scandal occurred when she cut off the head of her cousin, Mary, Queen of Scots (as a warning to everyone else). Lots of Catholics also lost their lives. (Why wasn't she called Bloody Elizabeth then?)

Elizabeth's fleet defeated the King of Spain's great Armada in 1588.

Bess (as her friends called her!) enjoyed Shakespeare's plays hugely (and his plays still plague schoolchildren today).

And what about Wales?

The poor old Welsh people didn't know which church – Protestant or Catholic – to support. Three Protestants were burned at the stake in Wales and several ran away to live on the continent. (The weather was a lot better in Switzerland, anyway!)

Then, in Queen Elizabeth's time, many Catholics ran away to the continent and the Protestants came home. These Protestants were determined to have Welsh-language services in the churches in Wales, and in 1588 (the same year as the Armada), William Morgan finished translating his famous Welsh Bible. (What a pity so few people could read!)

THE SLEAZY STUARTS

What happened in England?

JAMES I, who was also JAMES VI of SCOTLAND (1603–1625)
Elizabeth didn't marry or have any children, so the King of Scotland, the son of Mary Queen of Scots, was invited to rule Wales and England after she died. (Ha ha! Elizabeth!)

Guy Fawkes plotted to blow up Parliament – he wanted Catholics to have more rights – but he was caught and hanged (not burned!).

And what about Wales?

The Welsh people loved the Stuarts – because James's grandmother was the daughter of Henry VII, so he did have the tiniest fraction of Welsh blood in him. But James didn't do much (well, nothing to be honest) for Wales (except start Guy Fawkes night of course!).

We should have **burned** Guy Fawkes not hanged him!

CHARLES I (1625–1649)
Like his father, James, Charles believed God had chosen him to be king. So HE should rule the country NOT Parliament. He quarrelled with Parliament, a quarrel which started the Civil Wars between the Royalists and the Parliamentarians (1642–9). In the end, Charles was defeated and beheaded (poor old thing) at Tyburn, London.

Most of the Welsh people supported Charles and fought on the King's side in the Civil Wars. But one Welshman, John Jones of Maesygarnedd (yes, a Welshman called Jones!), signed the death warrant to behead the King in 1649 (he was a pigheaded man).

THE COMMONWEALTH PERIOD (1649–1660)
Parliament ruled without a king. (Well, he was dead after all!) Oliver Cromwell, the famous Roundhead general, was the new leader, and before long, he shut Parliament down and called himself Lord Protector of the Commonwealth.

Even though Oliver's great-great-grandfather came from Llanishen in Cardiff, the people of Wales didn't like him much, especially when he stopped them celebrating Christmas.

What happened in England?

When the Lord Protector (what a mouthful) died, his son, Richard (or Dick) became the ruler. But everyone grew fed up of Tricky Dicky, and he ran away.

CHARLES II (1660–1685)

Everyone was glad to see the 'Merry Monarch' crowned and to be able to enjoy music and plays again. He pardoned those who had supported Parliament, except those who had signed his father, Charles I's, death warrant. A dreadful plague and a huge fire swept through London in 1665–66. When he was dying, Charles became a Catholic again. (How sly, Charlie boy!)

JAMES II (1685–1688)

Charles II's brother and a Catholic. His nephew – the Duke of Monmouth – rose up in revolt against James. But the rebellion was a failure and the Duke had his head chopped off. James wasn't at all popular, and he had to flee to France. Parliament invited his daughter, Mary (a Protestant), and her husband, William of Orange, to come over to rule instead of James.

1688–89: THE GLORIOUS REVOLUTION

The end of the stunningly sleazy Stuart Age.

And what about Wales?

(No Santa, no tree, no presents – no fun – no thanks!)

Thank goodness. I can go back to sleep.

John Jones, Maesygarnedd, lost his head for signing the death warrant to behead Charles I. Now it was the Puritans' turn to be persecuted and some of them ran away for peace and quiet to live in America. (That was far enough away from the King's officers.)

Judge George Jeffreys came from the Wrexham area and HE was the one who kept law and order in the country and frightened James's enemies. After the Duke of Monmouth's rebellion, he organized the hanging of 250 rebels, and 1,000 people were transported overseas to the West Indies. Judge Jeffreys himself died in prison (serve him right!) after James had fled to France.

ᵗHE ᵗROUBLESOME ᵗUDORS:
ᵗHE HIDEOUS HEПRYS

1. HEПRY VII

A warm-hearted Welshman or one who broke Welsh hearts?

Historians are useless. They argue and quarrel all the time.

And what about the miserable history of King Henry VII (or Henry Tudor, as his mam called him)? Was he a good king for the people of Wales – or not?

Even those who were around at the time – or very nearly! – could not agree.

According to Siôn Tudor (no relative) who lived about a hundred years later than Henry:

Henry VII gave back their freedom to the people of Wales (not that they were actually in prison of course!).

But, according to Llywelyn (cry baby!) ap Hywel:

Henry likes the men of the north of England *better* than he likes the Welsh. Boo-hoo!

And historians are still arguing:

An English historian: Henry VII was the best thing to happen to Wales since sliced bread.

A Welsh historian: The Welsh people loved the Tudors, but did the Tudors love Wales?

Are you completely confused? Well, here's your chance to decide for yourself – after you've read Henry VII's hideous history. And here it is:

Who was Henry Tudor?
The Tudors' Formidable Family

Henry Tudor's grandfather – Owain Tudor – was quite
a Jack the Lad! He decided to leave his home in
Pen-mynydd, Anglesey, to make his fortune. (After all,
he couldn't have made much of a fortune on the top
(*pen*) of a north-Walian mountain (*mynydd*)!) He found
a job looking after the wardrobe of Queen Catherine
de Valois. (She was the King of France's daughter and
she had lots of clothes.) Her husband, King Henry V,
had died. One day, Catherine looked out of the palace
window and saw Owain Tudor swimming, naked!
She fell in love with him.

Oo la la!
Il est très
gorgeous!

Owain and Catherine got married and had several
children. One of them was Edmund Tudor, and he
married Margaret Beaufort (a good choice as she was
rich and clever, and she had a claim to the throne of
England). Margaret was only thirteen years old when
she gave birth to a baby son, Henry Tudor, in
Pembroke Castle. But her husband, Edmund, died
before Henry was born (very sad!).

These were troubled times, with one family – the House of Lancaster (the red rose), fighting against another family – the House of York (the white rose), for the crown of England.

These were the Wars of the Roses:

Henry's family belonged to the House of Lancaster (the red rose). During the bitter battle of Mortimer Cross, between Lancaster and York, Owain Tudor was caught and was about to be beheaded. Owain was a very proud man, and when his head was on the block, he said:

A horrible hag was watching the beheading. She took Owain's head, washed it, combed his hair and beard and put it on top of the market cross. Then, she lit 100 candles and placed them around the head.

There you are, love. You look more handsome now than when you were alive!

The Brilliant Battle of Bosworth

By 1485, King Richard III (from the House of York) was very unpopular. Many people wanted Henry Tudor to be king instead of him, but Henry was living in Brittany with his uncle, Jasper Tudor. They decided it was time to set sail to conquer England (and Wales). They came ashore in Wales first of all.

The Fabulous Fans

The people of Wales were delighted that Henry had arrived at last. They had been looking forward to having a 'Welshman' as king of Wales and England. They hurried to join Henry's army when it landed in Pembrokeshire. The poets had been writing clever poems telling everyone to support Henry. They wrote their poems in code, but unfortunately hardly anyone understood them (not even the poets themselves!).

Here is a snippet from a poem by Robin Ddu (the black robin). What a silly name – everyone knows a robin is red! Remember that it's in code and that the **bull** refers to Henry, and the **mole** represents Richard III, the bad king:

> *The time has come at long last*
> *For the **small bull** to venture out.*
> *The **mole** will fall from grace*
> *And be avenged – the world throughout.*

You don't understand it? (As I suspected!) Go and ask your teachers – they should be experts at writing things that are impossible to understand!

(You could try writing a poem in code about your school. What animals would you choose to represent your teachers, I wonder?)

THE JOURNEY THROUGH WALES . . . TO BOSWORTH

After landing in Pembrokeshire, Henry didn't go straight to England. He decided to travel north through Aberystwyth and Machynlleth (the scenic route!) before marching towards London.

Henry wanted to win over the most powerful leader in south Wales, Rhys ap Tomos, to join his army. BUT Rhys had promised King Richard III that he would only allow Henry to enter Wales over his body. So, what did Rhys do (according to the story, anyway)? He hid under a bridge to allow Henry and his army to walk over him! (Very clever, Rhys!)

On the way, near Machynlleth, Henry stayed at Mathafarn, the home of one of the passionate poets – Dafydd Llwyd (and his wife Margred) – who had supported him. Dafydd was one of Henry Tudor's fabulous fans and he had written fifty-nine poems saying that Henry would make a great king. But now, Henry asked Dafydd who would win the brutal battle – Richard III or himself?

Poor old Dafydd – he couldn't sleep a wink all night. What answer could he give Henry? Thank goodness – Margred was much cleverer than her husband.

Don't worry, Dafydd bach. Tell Henry that he'll win the battle. If he **loses**, he'll probably be dead anyway! If he **wins**, you're sure to be rewarded!

Thanks, love.

And away they all went to fight in the Brilliant Battle of Bosworth.

THE BRILLIANT BATTLE

on BOSWORTH FIELD, in the Midlands

22 August 1485

between

Richard III – King of England (House of York) (plus 12,000 soldiers)

and

Henry Tudor (nobody much – House of Lancaster) (plus 5,000 soldiers)

EVERYONE WELCOME!

But one brainy baron, William Stanley, had 4,000 soldiers, and he couldn't decide which side to support:

At the very last minute, wily William decided to help Henry. (After all, Henry's mother was his sister-in-law.) Richard was killed. Someone picked up Richard's crown and put it on Henry's head:

And now a Welshman (well, he was one quarter Welsh at least) was king of England and Wales. But how much of a Welshman was he? Did he do anything to help Wales?

Was he a warm-hearted king or a heartless one?

Priceless points FOR Henry VII:

✓ When Henry fought at Bosworth he flew the banner of the Welsh dragon. Hooray!

✓ After he became king he rewarded several Welshmen who had helped him by giving them important jobs – Rhys ap Tomos became Sir Rhys ap Thomas.

✓ Henry named his first-born son Arthur, after a great king in Welsh history. (But Arthur died when he was only sixteen years old, so he wasn't much help to Wales!)

✓ Henry gave money towards celebrating St David's Day in his court in London.

Prickly points AGAINST Henry VII:

✗ He was too busy running England to pay much attention to little Wales.

✗ He didn't do away with the laws which prevented the Welsh people from buying land and holding important jobs.

The FINAL SCORE: **FOR**: 4 **AGAINST**: 2

But, what do *you* think? Was Henry, the first of the troublesome Tudors, a warm-hearted Welshman or a king who broke Welsh hearts?

LAW AND ORDER

BAN THE BANDITS!

When Henry VII became king, Wales positively bristled with brigands who caused chaos and confusion throughout the land. Ysbyty Ifan in Snowdonia was as wild as a hornet's nest – full of ruthless robbers and marauding murderers. (Their story would make a much better film than Robin Hood!) Nearby, in the forest of Carreg Gwalch, lived the most outrageous outlaw in all Wales – Dafydd ap Siencyn and his bold band of bandits. If one of them had been able to send a letter home, this is what he might have written:

Carreg Gwalch Forest,
Llanrwst,
September 1482

Dear Mam,
I hope you're all right. Don't worry about me, your darling son. The cave where I live stinks and it's freezing here, but I'm having a great time with Dafydd ap Siencyn's brave bandits. Have you finished sewing that green tunic for me yet? Dafydd says we must wear green like the fairies. People are afraid of fairies, so they'll be frightened of us, too.

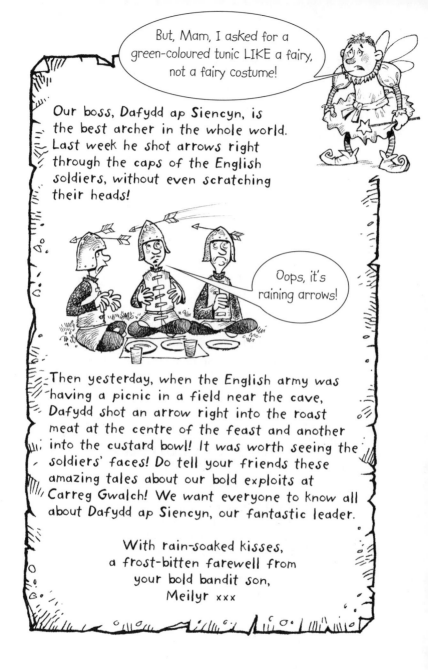

But, Mam, I asked for a green-coloured tunic LIKE a fairy, not a fairy costume!

Our boss, Dafydd ap Siencyn, is the best archer in the whole world. Last week he shot arrows right through the caps of the English soldiers, without even scratching their heads!

Oops, it's raining arrows!

Then yesterday, when the English army was having a picnic in a field near the cave, Dafydd shot an arrow right into the roast meat at the centre of the feast and another into the custard bowl! It was worth seeing the soldiers' faces! Do tell your friends these amazing tales about our bold exploits at Carreg Gwalch! We want everyone to know all about Dafydd ap Siencyn, our fantastic leader.

With rain-soaked kisses,
a frost-bitten farewell from
your bold bandit son,
Meilyr xxx

27

2. HENRY VIII

A BRUTAL BULLY

When Henry VII's son, Henry VIII, became king he wasn't prepared to take any nonsense from Wales. He wanted to outlaw every bold bandit and marauding murderer – for ever! He used two terrifying tactics to enforce law and order in Wales.

SHOCK TACTICS

Henry would hang or behead anyone – rich or poor – who dared to defy the king.

The Welsh people had a terrible shock when Rhys ap Gruffudd, the lord of Carew Castle, and one of Henry VII's best friends, was arrested, accused of treason and then – executed!

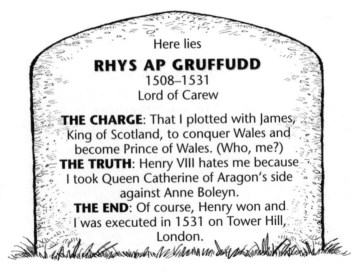

Here lies
RHYS AP GRUFFUDD
1508–1531
Lord of Carew

THE CHARGE: That I plotted with James, King of Scotland, to conquer Wales and become Prince of Wales. (Who, me?)
THE TRUTH: Henry VIII hates me because I took Queen Catherine of Aragon's side against Anne Boleyn.
THE END: Of course, Henry won and I was executed in 1531 on Tower Hill, London.

And so, dear friends:

> *Please meditate hard on my story,*
> *It's hardly a blueprint for glory,*
>   *So don't be a clot*
>   *And don't ever plot*
> *Against Henry the Eighth – it's too gory!*

(the headless) Rhys ap Gruffudd

The right-royal bully, Henry VIII, used Bishop
Rowland Lee to do a lot of his dirty work for him.
In nine years Lee succeeded in catching 5,000
criminals and he hanged them all. He enjoyed it so
much that he hanged one man who was dead already!

Welsh thieves were scared stiff even when they heard Rowland Lee's name.

Trick tactics

But in 1536 and 1543, Henry decided to try trick tactics against the Welsh people. He passed:

THE LAUGHABLE LAWS

These were laws or acts to UNITE Wales and England. Henry said he wanted to pass them because he 'loved Wales so much'! (Pull the other one, Henry!)

HENRY VIII'S LAUGHABLE LAWS

or the awfully silly Acts of Union, 1536 and 1543

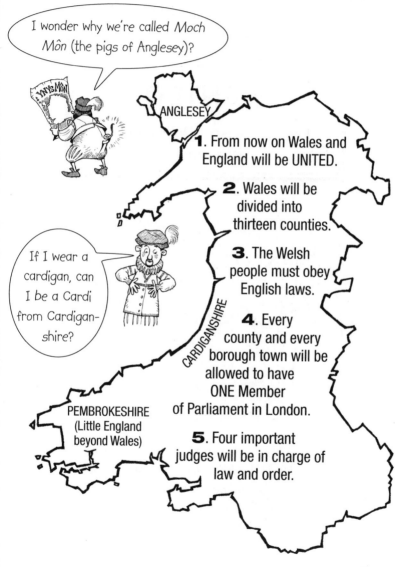

6. Any Welshman who wants an important job in Wales must be able to speak English.

Caernarfon Castle

WANTED

English speaker to look after the castle's prison.

Why do I need to speak English? The prison is full of Welsh people!

When once the new Acts became Laws,
The Welsh fell in love with each clause.
They changed overnight,
They agreed to unite,
And so freedom became a lost cause.

Some historians claim that the wicked Welsh changed overnight, from being bold bandits to being smug saints.

31 October 1536

Rhys Meurig from Glamorgan said:

And George Owen from Pembrokeshire claimed that:

The hearts of the Welsh people changed from wickedness to goodness, from bad to good.

UNFORTUNATELY, these pundits seem to have forgotten about some really terrifying troubles which occurred after the Laughable Laws had been passed:

A Pathetic Poem

The Mafia of Mawddwy

In Mawddwy in centuries past,
Brutal bandits marauded the land,
They were known to all of their neighbours –
Red hair was the badge of their band.

For Laws and for Acts and for Union,
For order, they cared not a toss,
'Cos the fierce Red Bandits of Mawddwy
Knew only too well who was BOSS.

After year upon year of marauding,
Of killing and threats without end,
The Sheriff of Mawddwy decided,
'It's time to clamp down on this trend,

'And I, Baron Owain of Mawddwy,
Will catch every one of this band,
And string them all up on the gallows,
No rogues will be left in this land.'

And the Baron he kept to his promise,
He hanged them with pleasure immense
As many as eighty Red Bandits,
He would hear not a word in defence.

A ruffian's mother tried begging:
'Please don't, Baron Owain! Oh no!
Don't hang Little Jack. He's my youngest,
My dearest one, please let him go.'

But the Baron ignored all her pleading,
Jack was hanged with the rest of his crew;
And his mother, in anguish and sorrow,
Shouted, 'I'll put my curse upon you.

'The loss of the least of my children
Will be fully avenged, believe me.
And his brothers will wash in your heart's blood
Right up to the elbow, you'll see.'

And so it occurred. One dark evening
As the Baron rode out through the land,
The bandits were waiting there for him
And shot him in face and in hand;

Then with thirty bold blows they attacked him,
Till he lay on the ground – dead as dead,
And the brothers, determined on vengeance,
Washed their hands in his blood, oh so red.

But that isn't the end of this saga,
Though the Mafia from Mawddwy all fled,
They were caught and eventually punished,
And hanged by the neck, until dead.

Then everything seemed to go quiet,
The band disappeared to thin air.
But they say that the bandits' descendants
Still inherit a mop of red hair!

The saga of Mawddwy's Mafia is so scary that lots of far-fetched fantasies, soppy songs and even films have been made about them. One local man from Mawddwy, Aneurin Brook, was chosen to act the part of a bandit because he had red hair. But the film was in black and white!

REGLIGION IN THE EARLY MODERN PERIOD

SQUABBLING, BICKERING AND QUARRELLING: ROUND ONE

During the Early Modern Period, there was more squabbling, bickering and quarrelling about religion than anything else. (How strange! Aren't religious people supposed to love one another?)

They were all CHRISTIANS, but in Henry VIII's time the church was split in two. This is what historians call:

The Protestant Reformation
CHRISTIANS

CATHOLICS
Catholics believe that the Pope in Rome is the head of the worldwide church. The Pope refused to allow Henry VIII to divorce his wife, Queen Catherine of Aragon, and marry his girlfriend, Anne Boleyn. (Catholics were not allowed to divorce.)

PROTESTANTS
Because the Pope refused to allow him to divorce Catherine of Aragon and marry Anne Boleyn, Henry VIII decided to break away from the Catholic Church and the Pope. He made himself the HEAD of the Protestant Church. He married Anne Boleyn (and then cut off her head!).

And that was the story of almost the whole of the Tudor Age – fighting and squabbling between Catholics and Protestants.

And during the Stuart Age – fighting and squabbling among different groups of Protestants (the Church of England, the Puritans and the Nonconformists). How confusing!

The history of the Tudors AND the Stuarts was full of hideous killing, burning and hanging.

BUT WHO WAS WHO?

THE CATHOLICS

We worship in the Church of Rome
Where saints and relics feel at home,
And Latin is the tongue we speak
When we attend the Mass each week.

Protestants – Church of England

We're Protestants. No Pope for us,
We like to worship without fuss.
The Church of England is our name.
*No Welsh? No Latin? What a shame!**

(*Later on the Protestants in the Church of England decided that the Welsh could have Welsh-language services.)

Protestants – the Nonconformists

We're Nonconformists. We decide
What's right for us. We can't abide
The Church of England, or the Pope:
The Bible is our only hope.

Protestants – the Puritans

We're Puritans: our name's the clue.
We're pure in all we think and do.
Our clothes are plain; our food is bland,
And we think Christmas should be banned.

Still completely confused? Read on to find out more about all this hideous holiness.

Step 1: Destroying every monastery

Throughout the miserable Middle Ages, the monasteries had been important in the history of Wales. But Henry's first step was to close them – ONCE AND FOR ALL.

Guess which FOUR RIDICULOUS REASONS
Henry VIII gave for closing the monasteries:

1. **He didn't support the monks'
   football teams.**

2. **The monasteries hadn't paid their
   rent.**

3. **There were only a few monks left in
   each monastery.**

4. **The monks didn't wash often enough,
   so the monasteries smelt awful.**

5. **The monasteries owned lots of land
   and wealth, and Henry wanted it all.**

6. **The monasteries were so far from
   everywhere that no one visited to
   say 'Hello!'**

7. **The abbots and the monks had
   completely forgotten their religious
   vows and they did whatever they
   wanted.**

8. **Henry wanted to turn the
   monasteries into luxury flats.**

9. **The monks were Catholics and
   Henry didn't like Catholics.**

ANSWERS:

3. According to the rules of the monasteries, there should be 12 monks (at least) in every abbey. But by Tudor times there were only 250 monks between all 50 abbeys in Wales (do your sums – that's 5 for each house). There was plenty of room in Tintern Abbey for 80 monks, but in 1536 only 13 lived there.

5. Henry certainly wanted to get his hands on the wealth of the great abbeys of England, but to do so he had to close the Welsh monasteries too. London's Westminster Abbey was worth £3,740 a year alone. The monasteries in Wales were worth only £3,178 ALTOGETHER! But the Welsh monasteries had a lot of land. Tintern owned 3,000 acres. Since Henry needed money to pay for his war against the King of France, he said: 'AWAY WITH THE ABBEYS!'

7. All monks were supposed to live good lives and keep their monastic vows:
   ✚ to live in poverty   ✚ not to marry and have children
   ✚ to obey the abbot.

   Henry sent a team of busybodies around the monasteries to find out whether the monks kept their vows or not. And what a surprise! It found some abbots and monks doing the strangest things:
   • Robert Salusbury, the abbot of Valle Crucis, near Llangollen, led a gang of highwaymen. He was caught and sent to the Tower of London.
   • Thomas Pennant, the abbot of Basingwerk, had left his abbey to get married and he had lots of sons.
   • Richard Smith, a monk at Strata Florida abbey, was accused of minting coins (making money).

Of course Henry made a lot of fuss about these men behaving badly.
He forgot to mention that many of the abbots and monks kept all their vows – yes, there were a few good men.

9. Yes, the monks were Catholics.

And FOUR RIDICULOUS REASONS were enough. By 1539 every one of the monasteries in Wales had been closed. (Bye bye, abbeys!)

But remember – they say that in Strata Florida the ghost of one poor monk appears on Christmas Eve every year to try to rebuild the abbey church.

STEP 2: WRECKING RELICS

Henry VIII's second step in conquering the Roman Catholic church was to organize a mighty binge of treasure trashing, relic wrecking and pilgrim bashing. How did he do it? Here are some of the steps that he took:

✚ The new bishop of St David's, William Barlow, told his cathedral canons (they were priests, not big guns!) to stop worshipping the two rotten skulls in the church, and to lock away Saint David's bones. (Cheerio, Saint David!)

✚ At Pen-rhys in the Rhondda there was a very famous statue of Mary, the mother of Jesus Christ. This was pulled down secretly one evening (in case the locals caused a fuss) and taken to London to be burnt with all the other curious Catholic relics.

Stop! Who goes there?

Mary, the mother of Jesus – but please don't tell anyone!

+ One of Henry VIII's servants found Malchus's ear in Bangor, north Wales. Malchus had lost his ear after St Peter cut it off, when he was defending Jesus about 1,500 years before the Tudor Age! How did Malchus's ear get to Bangor, I wonder? The ear disappeared after this and no one <u>heard</u> anything more about it!

I've never heard of Bangor!

+ In Llandaff Cathedral, Cardiff, there were statues of three saints – Teilo, Dyfrig and Euddogwy. The canons in the cathedral tried to hide them from Henry's snooping servants. But the servants found the saints' heads and destroyed them. Good gracious!

But the hideous history of St Derfel's statue is **the most famous** of all.

London's Loony Times

MAY 1538   1 penny

St Derfel's Statue - a FIERY END
Prophecy comes true!

THE CITY of London was on fire today as two vile villains were burnt alive at Smithfield. The hero of the hour was Dr Ellis Pryce who brought the first villain to London. 'The situation was disgraceful,' Dr Pryce told a reporter from *London's Loony Times*.

'When I was travelling around Wales trashing the monasteries, I happened to call at Llandderfel church in Meirionethshire. There I saw about 600 people worshipping St Derfel the Strong – praying to a wooden statue of an old Catholic saint on horseback – absolutely disgusting!'

Dr Pryce explained further that the gullible people of Wales believed that St Derfel's statue could prevent them from going to hell, after they had died.

Welcome to hell!

But I paid £6 to St Derfel to get me into heaven!

They were prepared to pay huge sums of money, and even give cattle and horses to the church, just so that they could see this statue. One of those who had made a pilgrimage to Llandderfel said, 'I have sinned dreadfully during my miserable life, but now, after seeing the statue of Derfel on his horse, I'm sure I shall go straight to heaven.' He donated £6 to the church.

The people of Llandderfel offered to pay an eye-watering £40 to save St Derfel's statue. But – it was too late! Dr Pryce tore the statue off its horse and brought it to London, to be thrown onto the bonfire. And this morning it was turned into ashes.

And the second villain on the bonfire? – Thomas Forest, a keen Catholic, who had been friends with Queen Catherine of Aragon.

A prophecy said that one day the statue of St Derfel would light up a whole **forest**. And so it did – because Thomas **Forest** burned on the same fire as Saint Derfel. *That was a good joke (but not for Thomas Forest, of course!).*

That's what I call a hot-headed Catholic!

(And then, they say, the Welsh began to worship Derfel's horse instead of the saint himself! Neigh!)

45

BUT ... even the Protestants couldn't destroy everything.

✛ They painted over the colourful pictures on the walls of some Catholic churches. But, recently, when experts were moving the church of Llandeilo Talybont from Pontarddulais to the National History Museum at St Fagans, they found these pictures once more! Now we can see them again. (Ha ha! Protestants!) And who do you think goes to see them in St Fagans? – Protestants of course!

✛ And the Welsh still believed strongly that the saints and their holy wells could cure all sorts of horrible illnesses.

This is how the churches might have advertised their relics, if there had been newspapers in Tudor and Stuart times:

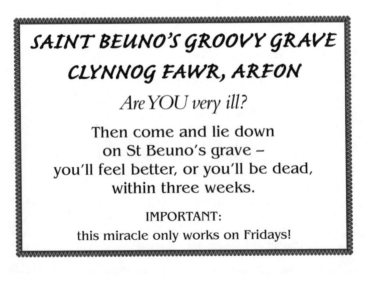

SAINT BEUNO'S GROOVY GRAVE
CLYNNOG FAWR, ARFON

Are YOU very ill?

Then come and lie down
on St Beuno's grave –
you'll feel better, or you'll be dead,
within three weeks.

IMPORTANT:
this miracle only works on Fridays!

Poor thing, he lay down on Beuno's grave on Wednesday instead of Friday!

†EGLA'S WONDERFUL WELL
LLANDEGLA

Do you suffer from Tegla's disease?

Then come and wash your feet and hands in Tegla's Well. Remember to bring with you a cockerel (if you're a man) or a hen (if you're a woman). Stick pins into the cockerel or the hen. (It doesn't matter if they're still alive – in they go!) Walk around the well nine times, reciting 'Our Father', before washing in the water. Then walk around the church three times. Put the bird's beak into the patient's mouth and sleep all night under the altar in the church. If the patient's skin is darker in the morning, he'll be cured. The disease will enter into the cockerel or the hen! Do remember to put money for the poor in the collection box, and leave the bird for the vicar (he loves chicken soup!).

THE MOST WONDROUS WELL IN WALES

GWENFFREWI'S WELL, HOLYWELL

*Are you: deaf? blind?
unable to have children?*

THEN GWENFFREWI'S WELL IS THE PLACE FOR YOU.
COME AND WASH IN ITS WATERS.

One of the Seven Wonders of Wales★

Sponsored by the royal family!
Margaret Beaufort (Henry VII's mam)
and James II and his wife, Mary.

REMEMBER TO LEAVE MONEY IN THE
COLLECTION BOX

[★ The wackiest wonder is that EACH ONE of the
Seven Wonders of Wales is in north Wales! Well, well!]

MARY'S MARTYRS –
HOLY SMOKE!

It's hardly surprising, therefore, that many Welsh people
were pleased when the Protestant king, Edward VI
(Henry VIII's son), died, and his sister, Mary Tudor –
a Catholic (she was Catherine of Aragon's daughter,
after all) – came to the throne.

BUT every hideous history book is full of scorching stories about Bloody Mary – the creepy queen who loved a good bonfire. In five years she burnt 283 passionate Protestants at the stake. (Perhaps she just couldn't afford a coal fire!)

In Wales there were only three martyrs:

- a fisherman called Rawlins White, in Cardiff;★
- William Nichol, in Haverfordwest;
- Robert Ferrar, Bishop of St David's, in Carmarthen.★★

★ Rawlins wrote to his wife before his final hour asking her to bring his wedding suit to the prison. He was burned at the stake in his wedding clothes. (What a waste of a nice suit!)

★★ Richard Jones of Abermarlais visited Robert Ferrar, the bishop of St David's, the evening before he was burned on 31 March 1555.

He might have described the evil event like this:

Today was a very gloomy day – the square in Carmarthen was chock-a-block with people, who had come to see the bonfire. I saw them tying the brave bishop to the stake and lighting the fire. It was slow to kindle, but the bishop didn't scream and hardly moved as the flames licked his legs and engulfed his body.

Bishop Ferrar told me last night that his bravery would prove that he was a good Protestant.

As he died he raised his arm aloft. It was like a bright candle. The square was as silent as the grave.

After this event the people of Carmarthen said that God sent a candle to warn every family when a member of that family was about to die. This was called a corpse candle. (You can read more about this under 'Curious Customs'.)

This Protestant was a real firebrand!

ELiZABETH I'S APPALLinG AGE (1558–1603)

After five years on the throne, Bloody Mary died and her sister Elizabeth became queen. And – yes, you're quite right – SHE was a Protestant! Poor people – in just thirty years they had to swing from one faith to the other – back and fore, back and fore, back and . . .

1530 ➜	1540 ➜	1555 ➜	1560
Catholics	Protestants	Catholics	Protestants

But at least Elizabeth was queen for long enough for the bewildered Welsh people to get their own Welsh-language Bible. (They couldn't understand a word of the English translation.)

William Salesbury was the first to try to translate the Bible into Welsh, with a little help from his friends – Bishop Richard Davies and Thomas Huet. They started with the New Testament. (Very wise move, because it's much shorter than the Old Testament.)

BUT when Salesbury's New Testament appeared in 1567, people couldn't read it. It was full of old-fashioned words and strange and mangled mutations (even at the best of times Welsh is a language of sudden and surprising spelling changes)!

Most Welsh people gave this New Testament only three marks out of ten.

Maurice Kyffin, a pompous Protestant, described Salesbury's efforts like this:

Welsh speakers can't bear listening to anyone reading Salesbury's translation.

And according to the gossips, William Salesbury and Richard Davies quarrelled so bitterly over the translation of ONE wretched word that the translation of the Old Testament was stopped in its tracks.

Isn't it lucky that there was someone else on hand to carry on the good work?

The sensational saint?

EVERYONE knows that William Morgan is a VERY, VERY IMPORTANT man in Welsh history. History teachers go on and on about this worthy Welshman who translated the Bible so magnificently. He's even had his picture on a stamp!

Here are some **Fantastic Facts** about this astonishing saint:

† William Morgan translated the Bible into Welsh in 1588.
† He could read and write five languages – Welsh, English, Latin, Greek and Hebrew (not many of these were of any use in Llanrhaeadr-ym-mochnant, where he was the vicar!).
† He spent a year in London making sure that the Bible was printed correctly.
† For all this hard work he was made Bishop of Llandaff and then Bishop of St Asaph's.
† The Bible helped to keep the Welsh language alive.

Quite a lad, then. BUT have your teachers told you THE WHOLE TRUTH about this brilliant (but belligerent) bishop?

EXCLUSIVE

More Fantastic Facts about (shaky) William Morgan:

† He quarrelled with his neighbour, Ieuan Meredith, of Lloran Uchaf, Llanrwst, all the time. Eventually Ieuan attacked William Morgan's home.

† Ieuan claimed that Morgan was threatening to burn down the homes of the people of Llanrhaeadr-ym-mochnant because they stole his firewood.

† William Morgan slapped his mother-in-law across her face. She was eighty years old at the time. He admitted that he had done so, but that the slap had done her good! (I wonder what she thought of that!)

† William Morgan hid two large guns under his long white gown when he took the services in church.

Heigh-ho! Heigh-ho! I'm the sharpest shooter in the west.

A sensational or a shaky saint? YOU decide. Perhaps he should have read the Bible more carefully when he was translating it!

Queen Bess's spiteful spies

Elizabeth I (Bess to her friends) had so many enemies that she needed spies everywhere. They searched homes – looking for Catholics under beds, in cupboards and even down the toilets. But it was very difficult to find the priests that came over to Wales from the continent to try to convert the Welsh back to Catholicism.

Several wealthy families helped to hide the priests down secret holes, where they could live for months if Elizabeth's soldiers were around.

In 1586, at Rhiwledyn on the Creuddyn estate, near Llandudno, eight Catholic priests succeeded in living for six months in a cave only five metres deep. In the cave they managed to print a Welsh book called *Y Drych Cristionogawl* (The Christian Mirror) – the first book ever to be printed in Wales!

But, very soon, these Catholics had been betrayed and the local magistrate, Thomas Mostyn, was on his way to the cave with an army of forty men to catch them. They watched the cave all night, but, when they entered it in the morning, the priests and the printing press had disappeared!

(What a shock for everyone! – but NOT, perhaps, for Thomas Mostyn, because secretly he supported the Catholics.)

Painful Persecutions

Not all Catholics were so lucky. Here is the horrific history of two Catholic priests who were hanged and drawn in good Queen Bess's reign:

1. **Rhisiart Gwyn** (or Richard White to the English)

Rhisiart Gwyn came from Llanidloes and he loved singing carols which said nasty things about the Protestants. He got on the nerves of Elizabeth's spies, so they arrested him time after time. (They weren't too keen on his singing voice either!)

In one case against him, the witness, a man called Lewis Gronw, had broken the law so many times that his ears were full of holes (that was one way of punishing criminals in Tudor times). During the hearing (!) the judge had to shout at Lewis all the time.

Eventually, Rhisiart Gwyn said, 'He should be able to hear better than anyone with all those holes in his ears!' (What a joke – no wonder the judge decided to hang Rhisiart!)

If one of those who watched the hanging had kept a diary, he might have described the sorry sight like this:

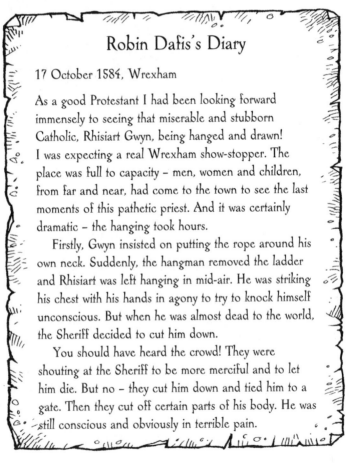

Robin Dafis's Diary

17 October 1584, Wrexham

As a good Protestant I had been looking forward immensely to seeing that miserable and stubborn Catholic, Rhisiart Gwyn, being hanged and drawn! I was expecting a real Wrexham show-stopper. The place was full to capacity – men, women and children, from far and near, had come to the town to see the last moments of this pathetic priest. And it was certainly dramatic – the hanging took hours.

Firstly, Gwyn insisted on putting the rope around his own neck. Suddenly, the hangman removed the ladder and Rhisiart was left hanging in mid-air. He was striking his chest with his hands in agony to try to knock himself unconscious. But when he was almost dead to the world, the Sheriff decided to cut him down.

You should have heard the crowd! They were shouting at the Sheriff to be more merciful and to let him die. But no – they cut him down and tied him to a gate. Then they cut off certain parts of his body. He was still conscious and obviously in terrible pain.

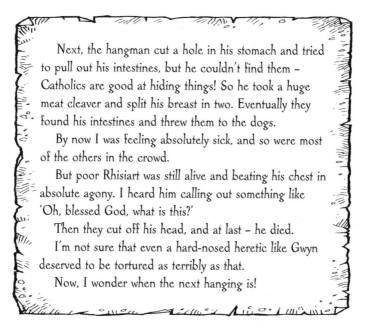

Next, the hangman cut a hole in his stomach and tried to pull out his intestines, but he couldn't find them – Catholics are good at hiding things! So he took a huge meat cleaver and split his breast in two. Eventually they found his intestines and threw them to the dogs.

By now I was feeling absolutely sick, and so were most of the others in the crowd.

But poor Rhisiart was still alive and beating his chest in absolute agony. I heard him calling out something like 'Oh, blessed God, what is this?'

Then they cut off his head, and at last – he died.

I'm not sure that even a hard-nosed heretic like Gwyn deserved to be tortured as terribly as that.

Now, I wonder when the next hanging is!

2. **William Davies**

The shocking story of the hanging of William Davies, one of the Catholics who escaped from Rhiwledyn cave, and who was executed in Beaumaris in 1593, is very similar. This time no one was willing to perform the atrocious act. Eventually, two men agreed to do the dirty work – for a huge fee. The children of the town threw stones at them.

William climbed the scaffold, made the sign of the cross and kissed the rope. When he was half dead, they cut the rope down. He was in immense pain, but they opened his body with a knife and tore out his heart.

57

Then they divided the body into four quarters and sent the pieces to hang in Conwy and Caernarfon castles. (This was a warning to the people NOT to cross Queen Elizabeth and the Protestants.) William's friends, Robert Pugh of Creuddyn and John Edwards, were keen to have a relic (something valuable) so that they would have a grisly souvenir to remember poor William.

ROUND TWO: page 125.

The curious customs of wicked Wales

If you want to make a (bad) impression on your hopeless history teachers (hopeless history not hopeless teachers), show them that you know all about the curious Welsh customs at the time of the troublesome Tudors and the sleazy Stuarts.

Groovy Greetings

During the Early Modern Period, the people of north Wales didn't say 'Hello' or 'Good morning' or 'Good afternoon' (like the polite people of south Wales). Oh no! When they spoke to their teachers they would use groovy greetings like:

Wala hi, Miss Jones!

Or, if they wanted to be even more groovy, what about these greetings?

'Cool, Mrs Williams!' or 'Greetings and nine curses to you, Mr Thomas!'

Unfortunately people liked to swear too – especially by using noisome names associated with dogs. They thought that dogs were noisy, nasty and quarrelsome creatures. (The RSPCA didn't exist at this time.) DON'T use these greetings – especially when you speak to your teachers:

You wouldn't have many friends if you behaved like that. But some Welsh speakers liked to use even more colourful greetings!

Do you know what these greetings mean? Let's hope not!

But here are some clues: *benglog (penglog)* = skull; *brwnt* = dirty; *hwch* = sow; *feddw (meddw)* = drunk; *lloercan* = lazybones; *bendew (pendew)* = thickheaded. As for the rest – least said, soonest mended!

Charming Love Charms

In wicked Wales during the age of the troublesome Tudors and sleazy Stuarts, girls wanted to find out who their sweethearts would be and who they would marry.

Here are THREE charms they used to raise their hopes:

Charm 1: Sweetheart cakes

The girls would mix the white of an egg with flour and salt; divide the mixture into two cakes; eat one cake and put the other cake under their pillow. Then, they would go to sleep. Their sweethearts would visit them, in a dream at midnight, to eat the other salty cake. This charm comes from Anglesey.

Ych-a-fi, I don't fancy this girl and her salty cake!

Charm 2: Slimy snails

A group of girls would come together to find white snails in the garden (have you ever seen a white snail?) and place each one under a bowl on a slate slab. Then they would go to bed and sleep. By the morning the snails would have written the first letter of the sweethearts' names, in their slippery slime, on the slate. Try this on Midsummer's Eve. This charm comes from Gwynedd.

But I can't write!

Charm 3: The love shoe

A girl would walk around a dung heap nine times,
carrying an empty shoe and saying,
'Here is the shoe, where is the
foot?' The sweetheart's ghost
would appear suddenly and
put his foot in the shoe
(the smelly Welsh version of
Cinderella!). Try this one on
Halloween –
31 October. This charm
comes from Ceredigion.

Ych-a-fi,
this shoe
stinks!

And if these charms
didn't work then the
poor girl would have
no husband at all
and would die a
spinster (very, very sad)!

Stupendous superstitions

In the Early Modern Period most wicked Welsh people
were stupendously superstitious.

The strange mermaid

In 1604, a number of villagers at Pendine,
Carmarthenshire, saw a creepy creature in the sea.
It looked like a mermaid, because it had the tail and
half the body of a fish, but it had a woman's upper
body and hair, and a dog's face! (Can you believe it?)

CORPSE CANDLES

People also believed that odd omens appeared to a family when one of them was about to die. Some would see a corpse candle, a small candle-shaped light, which came out of the mouth of a person who was very, very ill and about to die. This candle would travel slowly from the home of the sick person, along the path the corpse would be carried, and it would stop and stand still in the graveyard, at the exact spot where that person would be buried. According to John Davies, the vicar of Genau'r Glyn, Ceredigion, in 1656, everyone in that area could see corpse candles. Jane Wyatt, the vicar's sister-in-law, had seen five corpse candles on the same night that she stayed at Aberglasney Hall, Carmarthenshire.

This is the story she told the vicar:

It was a very stormy and windy night and I had gone to bed early. But in the dead of night I awoke suddenly. There was a very strange noise coming from the corridor outside my bedroom door. I didn't have a candle but I

 got up carefully and opened the door quietly. I was petrified when I saw five bright lights, like candles, in the corridor. They came out from under the door of the room where the maidservants slept. No one carried the candles but they moved very slowly along the corridor and out through the open window at its end. The window flapped back and fore in the wind.

I followed the candles quietly, with my heart in my mouth, and I saw them disappear up the narrow path towards Llangathen church. I was shaking like a leaf.

I couldn't sleep a wink all night after that.

But at about six o'clock in the morning I heard the sounds of shouting, screaming and crying. I ran out of my room and noticed that the door to the maidservants' loft was open. In the room I could see the five maids lying absolutely still, as white as sheets, dead in their beds.

Poor things. The day before they had been whitewashing the room and had lit a fire to dry the walls during the night. But the fumes from the whitewash had suffocated and choked them to death.

I didn't stay another night in Aberglasney Hall!

And they say that if you go to the churchyard in Llangathen today, you can see a row of graves in the exact spot where the corpse candles stopped that fateful night, to mark where the maidservants would be buried.

Four other curious customs – seen at funerals

 The Welsh people of the Early Modern Period loved a good funeral. The evening beforehand, they would hold a great party where they would eat, drink, be merry and play games. It was called a wake, though it wasn't meant to waken the dead!

 In Pembrokeshire, so they say, they played one ghastly game with the corpse itself.

Hirwen Gwd

You will need:

> one dead body tied up safely in a long white bag
> two muscular men
> a strong rope
> a big, open chimney place

When everyone was having lots of fun during the wake, one of the strong men had to climb up onto the roof of the house. Once there, he would throw a rope down the open chimney into the room where the corpse was lying. The rope would be tied soundly around the dead body. Then, the man on the roof would shout out, 'Are we ready to play?' and the man at the bottom would reply, '*Hirwen gwd*' (Long white bag).

And the corpse would be drawn up the chimney until its head popped out at the top!

No one knows why the people of Pembrokeshire liked this ghastly game – perhaps they just wanted to clean the chimney, but then the long white bag would become a long black bag, wouldn't it?

Have I reached heaven yet?

In 1666 a very sheepish law was passed. Everyone had to be buried in wool – after the sheep had been sheared of course! You had to have a certificate to prove that you had kept this law or you would have to pay a huge fine (huge by Stuart standards) of £5.

A Woolly Certificate

This certificate proves that

BAR-BA-RA BA-GLEY

from the parish of BA-LA, ME-EI-RIONETHSHIRE, was dressed in wool, and nothing but wool, to be buried.

Date: 1678.   *Witness: Bar-na-by Ba-gley*

Guess who thought up this sheepish law? Sheep
farmers and wool salesmen of course! Ba-a-a!

Shoo, sheep!
There's no room for both
of us in this coffin.

In funerals, two very unpleasant and ugly persons
would walk at the front of the procession from
the home to the church. They would be dressed
in black from head to toe – they wore black
gowns and hoods, black gloves, black shoes, and they
carried black banners. They were not allowed to speak
to one another, because they were the MUTES. Their
job was to frighten everyone and to make the funeral
even more scary and creepy.

You look like a hoody from hell!

Shut up!
You'll be the
death of me!

The important question after every funeral was 'Were there many people there?' Everyone wanted a VERY BIG funeral (well, not the dead person of course, because he couldn't care less!). One way to get a lot of poor people to attend your funeral would be to give each one a nice warm winter coat to wear. The only problem was that the dead person's initials had to be sewn on the coat because he'd paid for it (just like football sponsors, though of course they're not dead!).

When Richard Parry, Cwm, St Asaph's, died in 1649, fifty poor men were invited to his funeral and each one had a new coat with the letters R.P. on the back.

A year later they could have had another new coat if they had gone to Llandygái, near Bangor, to the funeral of the Archbishop of York, John Williams. It was almost like having a bus of supporters going from funeral to funeral.

Whose funeral shall we go to today then, boys?

Stupid Schools in Troublesome Tudor Times

Your school has probably got some ridiculous rules. But the rules in the stupid schools of Tudor times were much more ridiculous.

RUTHIN GRAMMAR SCHOOL RULES 1590

NO girls. (What a pity, or hooray?)
School starts at six o'clock in the morning. (Yawn!)
All hands and faces MUST be clean at all times.
NO going to the fair or the market in Ruthin.
NO playing with dice, cards or balls.
NO speaking Welsh.
Every small boy MUST speak English all the time (no Welsh).
Every big boy MUST speak Latin or Greek all the time (no English **or** Welsh).

But there were some interesting rules too:

> **Teachers are not allowed to beat boys on their ears, their eyes, their noses or their faces (but of course there are plenty of other places left – their bottoms, their legs, their backs . . .).**
> **NO maths lessons. (Hooray!)**

These rules were written for Ruthin Grammar School by a man called Gabriel Goodman. (Do you think he deserved the name Good Man?)

After leaving the grammar school, the sons of the gentry (rich people) would go on to university, either at Oxford or Cambridge (there wasn't a university in Wales). This is how William Wynn from Y Glyn, Meirionethshire, wrote to his son at Oxford in 1637. He wrote in English, although they both spoke Welsh.

Dear Cadwaladr,
Just a quick word as you begin your term in College. Remember to make friends with honest students who hate drinking and smoking (thanks for that awesome advice, Dad!). Don't speak Welsh with people who can speak English ... that's how you'll learn perfect English. I would prefer if you kept company with hardworking and honest Englishmen. Don't mix with the Welsh, who are lazier and more rebellious than the English. Be a good boy in College.
Love from your dismally dull dad,
William Wynn

Some snobbish Englishmen laughed at these Welsh-speaking university students. John Williams of Cochwillan describes how he blushed bright red (*coch*) when he spoke English, because everyone laughed at his Welsh accent (good thing that he lived at <u>Coch</u>willan then!).

WHERE WAS WHERE AND WHO WAS WHO IN WICKED WALES?

(Almost) everyone in the troublesome Tudor and sleazy Stuart ages believed that all people had their own special place in the world. God decided where that place was.

Imagine a school: the head teacher is on top, the teachers are in the middle, and there are lots of pupils at the bottom of the pile.

I'M the King of the castle and I'M the BOSS!

He thinks he's the HEAD and the BOSS BUT . . .

They think THEY are the bosses BUT . . .

But if this was turned upside-down – with the head teacher at the bottom and the pupils on top – the whole school would go HEAD over heels and the world would be TOPsy-turvy.

So, Who was Who

and

Where was Where

in the

Early Modern Period in Wales?

THE KING / THE QUEEN

THE NOBILITY
(There were only twenty very rich noble families in Wales)

★THE GENTRY★
(THEY were the important ones – they ruled the roost)

THE FARMERS
(Most of them lived on small farms which were quite poor)

THE WORKERS
(They were very poor and received tiny wages)

★★ THE POOR★★
(They were very, very, poor. Thousands of them roamed the countryside, begging and frightening the rest of the population)

★Seven tedious tests to prove that YOU are one of the JAMMY GENTRY★

1 You come from a superior family. If you can trace your pedigree (your family's hideous history) back for centuries, then you can claim to be one of the gentry.

My name is Huw, son of Siencyn, son of Jack the Lad, son of Adam, son of . . .

Well, well – what a rare breed!

2 You wish to turn your back on everything Welsh and to get on in the world by speaking English (rather badly) all the time (nothing new there!). Some of the gentry changed their wonderful Welsh names into posh English ones:

Bore da, Siôn ap Hywel!

John Howells to you, boyo!

3 You have grabbed as much land as possible by pinching it from your neighbours and stealing highlands and common land from the poor.

4 You hold as many important jobs as possible – sheriff, Member of Parliament, magistrate (to catch criminals). Here are some of the posts held by Sir John Wynn of Gwydir, Llanrwst:

> Member of Parliament for Caernarfonshire 1586–7
> Sheriff of Caernarfonshire 1587–8; 1603
> Member of Parliament for Meirionethshire 1588–9; 1600–1
> Member of Parliament for Denbighshire 1606–7
> He was made a Sir (knighted) in 1606.
> He was made a Baron in 1611.
> He died in 1627 – from total exhaustion!

5 You have built a grand and very fashionable mansion which has: glass windows (not paper ones); high chimneys; splendid fireplaces decorated with your family coat of arms; large bedrooms; and a long gallery to walk up and down during wet weather.

And you have filled the mansion with the latest furniture: tables and chairs (before this they usually sat on benches); a smart wardrobe (to hold all your best clothes); carpets; and a fabulous four-poster bed.

6 You spend your leisure time a-huntin', a-shootin', and a-fencin', or getting a famous artist to paint a portrait of you, and your wife and family.

7 You ALWAYS dress fashionably.

A Fashion Show: a gentleman and his wife in the troublesome Tudor age

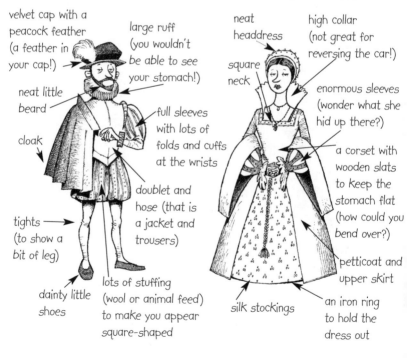

velvet cap with a peacock feather (a feather in your cap!)

neat little beard

cloak

tights → (to show a bit of leg)

dainty little shoes

large ruff (you wouldn't be able to see your stomach!)

full sleeves with lots of folds and cuffs at the wrists

doublet and hose (that is a jacket and trousers)

lots of stuffing (wool or animal feed) to make you appear square-shaped

neat headdress

square neck

high collar (not great for reversing the car!)

enormous sleeves (wonder what she hid up there?)

a corset with wooden slats to keep the stomach flat (how could you bend over?)

petticoat and upper skirt

silk stockings

an iron ring to hold the dress out

75

But by the Stuart Age the fashions had changed completely:

A Fashion Show: a gentleman and his wife in the sleazy Stuart Age

wig – from the hair of some dead person. It could cost £3 and some men cut off their own hair just so that they could wear someone else's!

wide sleeves full of folds and with cuffs at the bottom

very large collar – the ruff has fallen flat on the shoulders!

a high hat with a feather

high-heeled boots with neat little bows

tighter and longer trousers to show the shape of the leg (not great for fat men!)

hair in tiny little curls (they must have eaten a lot of crusts!)

lots of powder and make-up

large, grand collar

dress falling naturally without an iron ring to hold it out

a pomander full of perfume to keep bad smells, or the plague, away

76

In the Stuart Age, however, one group liked to dress very plainly in really boring clothes, in dark colours like black and grey. They cut their hair very, very short and in a circle on their heads. This is why these Puritans were called Roundheads.

Help! I look more like a Square-head than a Round-head!

★★ THE PITIFUL POOR ★★

At the very bottom of the ladder were the pitiful poor:

WITH NO HOME, NO WORK, NO FAMILY, NO MONEY, NO POSH CLOTHES

And there were thousands of them roaming the countryside. But where did they all come from?

- Some had been thrown out of the monasteries when they were closed.
- Some had been thrown off the common lands by the gentry and the farmers.
- Some had been injured in the army or at sea.

- And there were some who didn't want to work or lead respectable lives.

And the Government in England had the incredible idea that it should PUNISH every pitifully poor person.

The Loathsome Laws against the Pitiful Poor

1531: Every tramp must be caught, tied, stripped of his or her clothes and whipped through the streets of the town – that would teach them a good lesson!

1547: Every tramp (or Vagrant) must be branded by burning the shape of a V with a red-hot iron on the forehead (everyone would know him (or her) then!)

> Please can I have another letter? 'V' isn't in fashion this year.

1572: Any tramp who has broken the law must be whipped, his (or her) ear must be pierced, and the ear nailed to a tree.

In 1601 they decided there were three types of pitifully poor people:
  (i) young ones – they should work;
  (ii) the old and the sick – they had to go and live in almshouses or workhouses;
  (iii) lazy, bad ones – they should be punished and thrown into prison.

But the Welsh were quite kind to pitifully poor people. They allowed them to roam the countryside to beg for food and other goods.

A QUICK QUIZ ABOUT BEGGARS

Each form of begging had its own special name. What do you think a beggar would have come home with if he had gone out to:

(a) *glean* in the fields (*lloffa*)?
(b) collect *caws* (*cawsa*)?
(c) beg for *blawd* (*blawta*)?
(d) beg for *bloneg* (*blonega*)?
(e) gather *gwlân* (*gwlana*)?
(f) collect *calennig*?

Answers: (a) *lloffa*: to glean – collecting corn left behind on the corn field; (b) *cawsa*: to collect *caws*, cheese (to help the poor to dream); (c) *blawta*: to collect *blawd*, flour (to make pancakes); (d) *blonega*: to collect *bloneg*, fat or lard (*ych-a-fii*); (e) *gwlana*: to collect *gwlân*, wool (to knit socks); (f) to collect *calennig*: gifts of fruit and money on *Dydd Calan*, New Year's Day.

All Work and No Play in the Early Modern Period

The Dodgy Drover... and his Humble Apprentice

One thing the Welsh people were quite good at doing in the Early Modern Period was farming and rearing animals like cattle, sheep and pigs, and poultry, such as geese, ducks and hens. But because people were very, very, very poor, and although they were usually starving, they didn't eat these animals themselves. They walked them all the way to London to be sold. (And by then the animals were so thin they weren't much good at all!)

The farmers didn't drive the animals to London themselves. Oh no! They paid drovers to do this dirty and dangerous job. One Welshman, John Williams of Conwy (he became the Archbishop of York), said:

The drovers are the Spanish Fleet of Wales, bringing with them the little gold and silver we have.

(He was obviously a very bright bloke.)

Here is an extract from the imaginary diary of a drover's adventurous apprentice during the sleazy Stuart Age.

Monday 5 September 1635
Llangefni, Anglesey

Hooray, I'm going to escape from this horrible hole! I'm going to work as a drover's apprentice (a servant learning on the job) with Siôn Sais (they call him Siôn Sais – or Siôn the Englishman – because he's almost the only person who can speak English in Llangefni). I'll be helping Mr Sais drive his animals to London. And I started work today. Llangefni is 250 miles from London and we had to prepare the animals for the long journey by making sure they are properly shod. (No, not with shoes from a shoe shop!) What a spectacular sight: Huw the Blacksmith threw a rope around the two awesome bullock's horns, another man grabbed its legs and tripped it, so that it fell flat on its back! (Danger - Don't try this with a cow or a bull in a field, please!) Then they tied the bullock's legs together tightly and nailed shoes to its feet.

I love your new shoes!

Anyway I couldn't help with shoeing the cattle, because I was too busy shoeing the geese – nasty large white birds that hiss and bite. To be shod they were shod through hot tar which stuck to their feet. Then they walked through sand – and so, they had lovely new shoes for their long walk.

I've gone up in the world!

(Mum can't afford a new pair of shoes for me for the journey – I wonder whether I should walk through tar too?) I'm shattered now – roll on bedtime.

Wednesday, 7 September 1635
In a hedgerow, Bangor

A very strange day – the cattle, sheep and geese had to cross the Menai Straits. The cattle swam across. Siôn tied a rope around the first bullock's horns and the others followed it (they did the butterfly stroke most of the way!). Unfortunately, my boat was full of sheep and geese – in total panic. (I fancy a fat, noisy goose for supper tonight. Perhaps I'll go out in a minute with my sling and some lead bullets to kill one. I fancy a feather bed too!) It's high time someone built a bridge across the river Menai.

I'll have to wear a bikini next time!

Tuesday, 13 September 1635
Somewhere near Wrexham

I'm worn out and I'm fed up of this thankless, miserable work. Siôn Sais has a grand life, walking in front of the animals and calling in every pub on the way for a pint or two. He thinks he's Lord Muck when he calls out 'Haip Trwwwww . . . ww!' to the cattle. When people hear that call, they run to hide in their homes in case the animals charge them down!

But where do I and the rest of the drovers walk? Behind the animals. How would you like to look at the back ends of cattle and sheep all day, every day? And they are forever peeing and pooing. Just imagine how much pee and poo 200 cattle and 1,000 sheep can produce! And I have to walk right through it.

And on top of everything else, I have to sleep with the animals every night too, in the corner of a field or in a barn, to make sure that thieves don't steal them. The fleas and nits are eating me alive. Siôn sleeps in a comfortable bed in the pub, but I'm not even allowed in through the pub door because of the fleas and the smell. Everyone holds their noses when they see me coming.

There isn't much meat on this drover and he *stinks!*

Saturday, 17 September 1635
Somewhere in England

My boss is a very strange man. He must be quite
clever really, because he can write, and he has a licence
to say he's married and over thirty years old. BUT he's
also an incredibly miserly, mean so-and-so. There are
several toll-gates on the way to London, but Siôn won't
pay the tolls. Sometimes he makes us walk miles out of
the way to avoid paying them. You only have to pay a
toll for feet which touch the ground, so he makes me
ride a bullock, with a goose under each arm and a
sheep across my shoulders!

One ticket, sir?

And the roads are absolutely atrocious, full of holes and
puddles. There's no room for anyone to pass. The
Stagecoach and its snobbish travellers get very angry
when they are held up behind us, with the geese
dawdling along and the bullocks charging in front.
Someone should build a motorway to London!

A day off tomorrow because drovers aren't allowed
to travel on Sundays. Hooray!

Tuesday, 20 September 1635
On the Welsh Road to London

An extremely exciting day! We were stopped by a
highwayman! I'm not very sure where exactly –
Wolverhampton? . . . or Dunstable? . . . these English
place names are so difficult to remember. But suddenly
this threatening thief, riding a huge black horse,
appeared from behind a tree. He had a gun and he
shouted 'Stand and deliver – your money or your liver!'
The cattle didn't understand him of course and they
walked straight on. Poor old thief! We didn't have
any money at all, not even Siôn Sais, because we were
on the way to London, to sell the animals, and not on
the way home with the cash. Two of the dodgy drovers
had hidden among the cattle. Suddenly they jumped up
and targeted the thief with a lead bullet from their sling.
He fell to the ground like a sack of potatoes and Siôn
Sais ran up to him and shot him dead in his head with
his own gun. (That highwayman won't trouble any more
travellers!) We left the body where it fell, to be eaten
by the animals of the forest, but we took his horse
and saddle to sell in London. I hope I have a share of
this loot.
  I don't think I'll be able to sleep tonight after all
that drama.

Friday, 25 September 1635
Near London

Nearly there, thank goodness. To be honest I've had a
gutsful of this dirty, stinking, dangerous work.

I never want to be a drover's apprentice again and I don't even want to see London. The problem with London is, it's so far from everywhere – well, at least, from Llangefni!

And I've heard a rumour that Siôn Sais, our 'respectable' drover, intends to steal the money he gets in London for selling the animals, and escape to Ireland. (He'll be Siôn the dodgy Irishman then, not Siôn the dodgy drover! And what about his poor wife?)

I'm going to start walking home tomorrow – only 250 miles to go. Goodnight, all.

DID YOU KNOW THAT?

Jaw-dropping facts about work ... work ... work:

1. The sheep of the Early Modern Period were the first punks? The fussy farmers cut weird holes in their sheep's ears so that they knew which ones were theirs. And these holes had the strangest names, such as: *toad's-tongue; hole-in-the-heart; short-horn-prickle!*

What kind of hole would you like today, madam?

Oh! I'll have a toad's tongue, please!

2. According to a German wire maker called Schutz, the Welsh people of Tintern, near Newport, were useless employees. Schutz came to the area to run a wire-making business in 1566. He said, 'The Welsh are such hopeless workers – they don't do any good work at all!'

Schutz lost £800 (a lot of money at this time) during his first year in business, because, he claimed, the Welsh were so dull. But he must have changed his mind by 1603, because 600 Welsh people were working for him, and a further 10,000 were using wire to make other goods. By this time he was a very wealthy man. (Thanks to the 'stupid' Welsh!)

3. In Pembrokeshire, little boys had to work underground in the coalmines. Their job was to carry between eighty and one hundred casks of coal a day, from the coalface to the surface, on their backs. There were many nasty ways for little boys to die in the mines. Sometimes:
- soil fell on them and they suffocated;
- the pits were flooded and they drowned;
- they were choked by noxious gases.

How tragic!

How would you like to die, *bach*?

4. When someone tried to open a mill to smelt lead in Holywell in 1589, the local squire, Piers Mostyn, was very angry. He didn't want smelly works near his magnificent mansion! And the people of Holywell agreed with him. They didn't like all the pollution killing their cattle and polluting the river. They attacked the mill several times and destroyed it. Eventually, the people of Holywell won their battle. (<u>Well</u> done!)

Wicked Wales's Wondrous Women

Have you noticed anything peculiar about the hideous histories in this book – so far? Most of them are about MEN having lousy lives. But women's lives could be even lousier – especially if they were married.

For better or for worse?

When Jane Owen from Pembrokeshire married, in about the year 1600, her father gave her husband, David Lloyd of Carmarthenshire, a huge sum of money. This was a very useful custom if you had an ugly daughter and you wanted to get rid of her. But David Lloyd wasn't happy. He had hoped he would get a lot of land too. And so, in a fit of temper, he attacked his new wife. He threw her down the stairs, split open her head with a club, wounded her with a sword, smashed four of her teeth and pulled her hair out in large chunks (all for a bit of land!). We don't know whether he was punished, or not, for being such a monster.

Punishing a scold

If a wife moaned, scolded or nagged her husband all the time, he could punish her by putting her head in a scold's bridle. This was an iron frame, which fitted like a cage around her head. It had a piece of metal, or a 'bit', which went into the wife's mouth.

As a result the scold couldn't move her tongue, and she certainly couldn't moan or nag him any more.

Mm-mm . . . goo-goo . . . burn . . . hang . . .

Pardon? Did you say something, darling?

SELLING A SPOUSE

When they couldn't stand being married any more, some husbands tried to sell their wives, like animals in a livestock market. Sam Tŷ Cornel wanted to sell his wife, Mari Griffith, at Llanybydder market in around 1700. Sam told his audience all about her. Because he really wanted to get rid of her, he described her like this:

She's a wondrous wife – she can make tasty butter, she can sew, spin, bake, milk, laugh, sing tunes and read. BUT she is also a mouthy moaner, a quarrelsome liar who whines and scolds me all the time – (boo-hoo!). Is anyone willing to offer me £3 for her, please?

At last Siaci Llwyd, Tŷ Simnai, Carmarthenshire, paid just £1 for her (was that a bargain, I wonder?).

Good will?

But it wasn't always possible to escape, even when your husband had died:

The Will of John Glynne, Plas Newydd, Llandwrog, 1681

I, John Glynne, the squire of Plas Newydd, bequeath £600 (a lot of money in Stuart times) to my dear wife. BUT if she remarries anyone else called Glynne, she can't have a penny of this money.

But some wives managed to cope very well indeed:

A gallery of wondrous wives

Married four times!

Margaret Beaufort (1443–1509)

Husband No. 1: Margaret was only seven years old when she married a little six-year-old called John de la Pole (a toy boy?).

Husband No. 2: Then she decided she preferred Edmund Tudor. Before she was fourteen years old she had married him, she had a son called Henry (later Henry VII), and poor old Edmund had died!

Husband No. 3: Henry Stafford – he died.
Husband No. 4: Lord Thomas Stanley.
Margaret only ever had one child and he
was the apple of her eye. She plotted and
plotted to ensure that he would become
king of England and Wales in 1485.
Margaret was an extremely wealthy

woman, but towards the end of her life she decided to
live like a nun and wear a shirt of goat's hair next to
her skin – to itch and scratch her. (Perhaps she'd had
enough of men by then.) Although Margaret Beaufort
was an Englishwoman, she was the mother of Henry
Tudor and his most fanatical fan, so she's important in
the hideous history of Wales too. What a legend!

Catrin of Berain (1534–1591)

Husband No. 1: John Salesbury of Lleweni – by 1566
he was dead.

Husband No. 2: Sir Richard Clough from Denbigh – a very successful merchant in Europe. He built a grand brick mansion, like the houses in the Netherlands, in Bachegraig, Tremeirchion. But the local people thought the design was a very strange one and that the Devil had built it. According to one story, Sir Richard liked gazing at the stars through a small window in the roof of his mansion, and that he went there to speak to the Devil. One day, Catrin spied on him and the Devil disappeared in a puff of smoke. Another story claims that Catrin attacked her husband and that blood spurted all over the walls of their bedroom. They say that even today it's impossible to clean the bloodstains from the bedroom walls. Sir Richard died abroad in 1570, but his right hand and his heart were returned in a silver casket to be buried at Eglwys Wen, Denbigh.

Shall I gift wrap any other part of the body?

Husband No. 3: Maurice Wynn of Gwydir. According to legend, he asked Catrin to marry him when she was leaving her first husband's funeral.

Husband No. 4: Edward Thelwall, Plas y Ward, Denbigh.

He'll be really hard of hearing now!

But how many husbands did Catrin actually have? After she died, many remarkable rumours began to circulate about her. They said that she had married eight times and that she had killed all her other husbands by pouring lead into their ears – and that they were all buried in the orchard at Berain. (But historians, who like 'the whole truth', doubt whether these strange stories about Catrin of Berain are true.)

Altogether Catrin had lots of children and step-children. She was related, they say, to everyone of any importance (even distantly to Queen Elizabeth herself) and so, she has been called *Mam Cymru* – the Mother of Wales.

THE SCANDAL OF THE LITTLE LADY: AGNES NEEDHAM FROM SHROPSHIRE

A detective story from the Early Modern Period!

Agnes was the second wife of Sir Richard Bulkeley of Anglesey. When he was away, as the Member of Parliament in London, around 1570, Agnes had a great time with three other men. They sang beautiful songs to her under the eaves of her bedroom window. After Sir Richard returned home, he became very ill – he had diarrhoea and blisters appeared all over his legs. Within three months he was dead.

But how? Had the Little Lady been putting poison – arsenic or mercury – in his drink? When they came to search the mansion they found white powder hidden in a piece of paper in the Lady's velvet footwear. (What do you think – does this seem rather **slipper**y behaviour?) Luckily for Little Lady Agnes, in spite of the white powder, she wasn't charged with murder.

> Mmm . . . they both sound very tasty!

> Arsenic or mercury-flavoured beer, darling?

If you were found guilty of poisoning someone during the Early Modern Period you could be boiled alive in oil!

> Help! I didn't realise that they had chip shops in Tudor times!

Double, Double, Toil and Trouble
Wicked witches in Tudor and Stuart times

The people of the Early Modern Period were very, very frightened of witches. Parliament passed several loathsome laws to catch and punish them. Thousands of witches were burned and executed.

A TABLE OF WITCHES WHO WERE PUNISHED AND BURNT

Europe:	100,000
Scotland:	about 4,500
England:	about 300
WALES:	only about 5

So, Wales was at the bottom of the leader board. (Well done, Wales!)

If you had lived at this time, the following advice would have been very useful:

HOW TO RECOGNISE A WITCH (*if you met one in the street*):

- she would be a woman – a hideous old hag, with cross eyes, a hairy lip and a squeaky voice (not many men were witches, however ugly they were);
- she would live in a remote spot, far away from other people;
- she would have a black cat or a yellow frog.

Gwen the daughter of Ellis from Denbighshire was accused of witchcraft in 1595, because she had a remarkably large fly in her house. They said it was the Devil. Gwen was hanged for being a witch.

I wonder why they thought I was the Devil.

Other terrifying tests to catch witches:

1. Swimming a Witch: Firstly, they tied the thumb of the witch's right hand to the thumb of her left foot, and the thumb of her left hand to the thumb of her right foot. Then they threw her into a pond. If she could swim, this proved she was a witch and could be burnt at the stake or hanged. If she sank, she wasn't guilty – but she'd drown anyway!

She was a bit of a handful, wasn't she?

OK, OK, I admit I'm a witch!

2. **DUCKING A WITCH**: They tied the witch onto a ducking stool at the end of a long pole. Then they ducked the poor thing up and down in a deep pool of water until she confessed she was a witch – or died, of course. In Dolgellau, this stool was called *Y Gadair Goch,* (the Red Chair) and there was a pool in the river Wnion where they would duck ugly old women regularly.

How to keep a Witch away:

 Carry a piece of rosemary, thyme or lavender under your nose.

 Plant a holly bush or a rowan tree in front of your house. The red berries will keep evil spirits and witches away. (Unfortunately, they'll take at least twenty years to grow.)

 Make the sign of the cross.

Make the shape of a circle around your nose.

How to bewitch another person (*or how to put a nasty spell on someone – DON'T try these in school*):

 Get hold of a piece of the hair or nails of the person you want to bewitch. Put it in some wax and make the shape, or an image, of that person. Then, stick pins into it. Bad luck will surely follow. Tangwystl, the daughter of Glyn, was accused, in 1500, of bewitching John Morgan, the Bishop of St David's, (a very important man) by using this spell. The bishop had tried to stop Tangwystl's affair with a wealthy married man. She was supposed to have been brought before the court for bewitching the bishop, but he died very suddenly. Wicked!

 Find a live frog and stick pins in it. Then put it in a cauldron with a slate lid on top. Write the name of the person you wish to bewitch on the lid. This is a very successful spell.

 Curse someone by shouting out ghastly greetings. Elizabeth Parry from Denbigh tried this spell. One day she saw a woman milking and she shouted 'The Devil blesses your work'. With that, the cow fell on top of the woman and she was almost crushed to death.

99

How to Unbewitch (*undo a spiteful spell*)

† Make the sign of a cross in the dust at the witch's feet and spit on it (on the sign not on the witch!).

Abra-cad-abra . . .

Pah! . . . Stop it!

† Beat the object that has been bewitched hard with the branch of a hawthorn bush (unfortunately the hawthorn is full of nasty little thorns).

Two Crazy Cases of Bewitching

THE TRUTH and nothing but THE TRUTH? (*YOU decide*.)

1. In a Law Court in Flintshire in 1657

Judge: What is the name of the accused?

Ann: Ann Elis from Llannerch Banna. I'm very poor, sir, and I live by knitting stockings and begging around the farms.

Witness 1: Ann Elis soured the butter I was churning because I refused to give her any money.

Ann: But the butter had gone sour because of the hot weather, sir.

Witness 2: Ann Elis made my daughter ill by cursing her, sir.

Ann: But all I did was shout at her because she had stolen bread from my house. I'm so poor.

Witness 3: Ann Elis has brought bad luck on my son, Richard. He's become lame all of a sudden. And he's such a good boy.

Ann: Such a good boy! He climbed onto the roof of my poor little cottage and used the chimney as a toilet! And he became lame after falling when he was playing ball, not because of anything I said. Honestly, sir.

Witness 3: Well, perhaps he isn't a saint, but she did bewitch him – you've got to believe me.

YOU be the judge. Was Ann Elis guilty and did she deserve to be punished by hanging or burning?

(The court decided to send her to prison, but later she was released. Perhaps they couldn't decide either!)

2. Guilty without a Trial

The fate of Dorti Ddu, a huge hag from Llandecwyn, Meirionethshire, is enough to frighten you out of your wits.

The local people were fed up of Dorti Ddu and her stupid spells – turning butter and milk sour, making people and animals ill, cursing and swearing at everyone. And so, they decided to punish the wretched witch themselves, without taking her to court.

They dragged her to the top of a cliff above Lake Tecwyn. They threw her into a cask and punched long nails into its sides. Next they sealed it tightly. Then, they threw the cask (with poor Dorti in it), over the side of the cliff into the lake. The cask fell and smashed into tiny pieces. Dorti's body lay shattered and splattered at the bottom of the cliff. Her tongue would never cast a spell again!

This will be the last nail in my coffin!

In 1735, Parliament passed a law which stopped the persecution of witches and innocent old women.

Fair Play, or Foul?

When the foolish ordinary folk weren't killing themselves working, they were killing themselves, or other people, by playing all kinds of dangerous and sweaty sports.

Take care if you intend playing any of these!

Cnapan

This wacky game was a favourite with the foolish folk of Pembrokeshire:

You'll need:

- no rules
- no referee
- two teams of any number of players; men and women, on horseback or on foot. (Sometimes, 1,500 players would join in this groovy game.) You can throw or kick the ball (and kick the other team too!).
- dress code: men – trousers only; women – in petticoats
- a round ball – the *cnapan* – a piece of wood which has been boiled in wax until very slippery, or a cow's stomach filled with air. (Not a live cow, of course!)

The winning team is the one that can carry the *cnapan* so far away that it can't be retrieved by nightfall.

One bright spark described this groovy game:

'Some break their necks, some their backs, some their legs, some their arms. And blood flows from their noses, and their eyes are almost popping out of their heads. Hair and beards (the men's, of course) are pulled without mercy.'

What fun, don't you think?

I wish they'd asked my permission before taking my stomach!

CLiMBiNG A GREASY POLE

You'll need:
- two long poles covered in goose or pig fat to make them very slippery
- two men to compete to be the first to climb each pole.

Everyone kept away from these two men when they'd finished, because they smelt awful!

What a feat, don't you think?

But the most popular Welsh sports during the Early Modern Period were the gruesome games played by taunting animals and birds.

Baiting a Bull

You'll need:
• a big, beefy bull in a bad temper
• a huge dog (a mastiff if possible) in a worse temper.

And there you are – bring these two together within a circle and let them fight. Sometimes the bull would throw the dog high into the air on its horns, breaking the dog's back as it landed. The game ended when the bull or the dog was near to death, and there was blood everywhere.

How sporting is that?

Cockfighting

You'll need:
• two brave cockerels in a bad mood
• a cockpit or a graveyard in which to hold the contest.

Before a fight the cockerels' owners would:
• cut the cockerels' combs (not their hair combs – a cockerel has feathers not hair!), because if they were torn during the fight there would be a bloodbath
• put the cockerels on a diet so that they were fit and strong

I hope I look cute for the contest!

• tie spurs (metal spikes) to the cockerels' legs.
Then, everyone would take a bet on the winning
cockerel. The cockerel still alive at the end was the
CHAMPION.

If a clever cockerel ran away and refused to fight, then
it would be killed and eaten anyway.

So everyone was cock-a-hoop!

Threshing the Hen

This was a spiteful sport played on Shrove, or Pancake,
Tuesday. To make pancakes you need eggs, and if a hen
hadn't laid an egg, then it had to be punished.

You'll need:
• a hen which hasn't laid an egg
• men wearing masks and carrying sticks.

During this 'sport' the hen was tied to a pole in the
middle of a field. Then the men tried to hit, or thresh, it
with sticks. The one who killed the hen could have it
for supper.

Ha! ha! I prefer
Blind Man's Buff!

There's **hen**-tertaining, don't you think!

Hunting the Wren

You'll need:
- a little wren – but you must hunt it first
- a wren house made of wood and decorated with ribbons
- a group of youths to carry the tiny house around the area and to sing.

Sometimes the young men would kill the wren and divide its body amongst their friends. Then they would sing this squeamish little song:

> *A leg for Dibyn and a leg for Dobyn,*
> *A wing for Richard and a wing for Robin,*
> *Half a head for Siôn at the end of the street,*
> *And half a head for anyone else we may meet.*

They liked playing this 'sport' at Christmas time. How very festive!

But not every sport was as cruel or bloody. Here are some games you could try at home:

Throwing Quoits

You'll need:
- a piece of iron stuck into the ground
- a horseshoe (please remember to take it off the horse first!).

Everyone stands some distance from the iron and tries to throw the horseshoe around it. You can create your own scoring system.

I wish they would read the rules before starting to play!

Playing Dice

You'll need:
- two dice
- people who can count to twelve
- any number of players.

Throw both dice together – the one with the highest total number will be the winner.

People liked to bet on the winner and often this would lead to a fight.

In 1590, Gruffudd ap Gronw was arrested in Wrexham fair for hiding two dice down his trousers in a very dodgy place!

A Gurning Competition

You'll need:
- lots of really ugly, repulsive-looking people, or persons with 'elastic' features, to compete at making frightful faces!

The one who can pull the ugliest face is the winner. (You could think about the most hideous history lesson you've ever had – it would certainly help.) But you must be careful, or your face might stick like this forever and ever.

I told you not to compete!

A Tournament

Rich people had their own 'sport'. They killed one another in tournaments.

In 1507, Sir Rhys ap Thomas, of Carew Castle, Pembrokeshire, organized a tremendous tournament to

celebrate the fact that the king had made him a 'Knight of the Order of the Golden Garter' (the golden garter was a ribbon worn around the thigh).

About 600 people came to the great feast and they ate, drank, hunted and fought for five days.

The highlight of the feast was a play in which Saint David (the patron saint of Wales), walked up to Saint George (the patron saint of England), and hugged him warmly. This was meant to show that Welsh people, like Sir Rhys, were prepared to be friends with the English, at last.

After this pretty little play the knights went back to fight, injure, and half kill one another in the tournament.

Let's make the Punishment fit the Crime

During the Early Modern Period they enjoyed thinking up weird ways to punish anyone who had committed a calamitous crime – anyone who had broken the law – whether their crime was BIG or small.

You can try to be a Justice of the Peace (a person in charge of law and order), and you can decide which painful punishment fits which crime.

CALAMITOUS CRIMES	PUNISHMENTS
1. 1556: Lowri, daughter of Rhys of Betws – accused of stealing a loaf of bread and 6 cheeses, the property of Lewis ap David.	**A.** Hanged
2. 1550: a nobleman called Morris ap Eliza of Clenennau – accused of stabbing Robert ap Gruffudd with a sword until his brain spattered out in all directions. Robert died. Therefore, this was murder.	**B.** Put in a scold's bridle (an iron frame placed around the head with a piece of metal going into the mouth to prevent the tongue from moving).
3. 1557: Margaret, daughter of Ieuan of Ffestiniog – accused of stealing a cheese worth 1p, and 2p in money, the property of Lewis ap Siôn of Clynnog.	**C.** Put in the stocks.

Calamitous Crimes	Punishments
4. 1577: Lewis ap Gruffudd – caught begging in Monmouth.	**D.** Whipped from one town to the next.
5. 1597: John Clerk of Calcot, Flintshire – accused of stealing one animal every week.	**E.** Between 10 a.m. and 1 p.m. they took off the clothes from the upper part of her body, tied her to a horse and cart and pulled her along the town's High Street; she was whipped from Porth yr Aur to Porth Mawr until her body was blood-stained. Then she was put in the pillory.
6. 1541: John ap Dafydd of Caernarfon – accused of trespassing on Richard ap William's land in Bangor at night and stealing 5 waggonloads of hay, worth 20p.	**F.** Hanged.
7. 1563: Robert ap David of Caernarfon – accused of stealing a measure of lime worth 10p.	**G.** Tied to a piece of wood shaped as a T; whipped and flogged.

CALAMITOUS CRIMES	PUNISHMENTS
8. Margaret, a maid servant at Ynyscynhaiarn – accused of swearing on a Sunday.	**H.** Whipped and then nailed by the ear to a pole in the town's market place.
9. 1686: Grace Rowland – accused of stealing a sheep worth 4 shillings.	**I.** Pardoned by the king after paying a huge sum of money for his freedom.
10. 1649: Elin Hughes of Caernarfon – accused of moaning and nagging everyone endlessly and causing trouble among the townspeople.	**J.** Put in the pillory with a note pinned to him to say what he had done.

What kind of Justice of the Peace did you make? Let's hope you were really cruel and that you gave punishments that fitted the crimes.

1 and D: The troublesome Tudors liked to whip and flog calamitous criminals.

2 and I: Only wealthy people, like Morris ap Eliza, could afford to pay huge sums of money to buy the king's pardon. And as it so happened, his father, Eliza, was a Justice of the Peace too! (Fair play?)

3 and H.

4 and G: Begging was considered a dreadful crime in the Elizabethan Age, especially if you were a healthy young man who could work.

5 and A: Stealing animals was a popular and very dangerous hobby in the countryside (there was nothing better than eating the evidence for supper!).

6 and F.

7 and J: Standing in a pillory with your head and arms stuck into tiny holes could be extremely miserable. If you were there for hours, your body would tire and begin to sag. Then your neck could snap in half – and you would die.

8 and C: The stocks, which imprisoned your hands and feet, were not as cruel as the pillory, but people would enjoy mocking and laughing at you. They would throw all kinds of stinking and unpleasant things, like rotten eggs or potatoes or even pee and poo at you. In Dolgellau they had two sets of stocks – one was on wheels, so that the calamitous criminal could be paraded around the town. (There must have been some very bad people in Dolgellau – in the past, of course!)

9 and E.

10 and B: Scold's bridle – more about this and about nagging and moaning women in 'Wondrous Women'.

Not many people were imprisoned for long periods (not like today) during the Early Modern Period and there wasn't much room in these old prisons. A prison keeper could be punished by hanging if any of the prisoners escaped. So he always made sure that every prisoner was shackled and handcuffed securely.

But in 1589 a woman walked out of Denbigh prison with shackles on her legs. She visited the town market, stole a piece of cloth, a brass bowl and a pig and then ... she walked straight back into the prison! The keeper was obviously delighted to see her returning!

One peculiar problem facing every crafty criminal was that the official language of the law courts in Wales was English (this was one of the laughable laws of Henry VIII). The criminals couldn't understand what was being said about them in court, or what their punishment was going to be!

For stealing a sheep – hanging by the neck until dead!

Thenciw, syr, diolch yn fawr *iawn*, syr!

But some hideous historians claim that far more Welsh was spoken in the law courts than we imagine because otherwise it would have been impossible to conduct any business at all. Some lawyers were very good at deceiving Justices of the Peace who didn't understand Welsh.

Sailing Close to the Wind

The sea has always played an important part in the hideous history of Wales.

Unfortunately, though, very few exciting explorers or sailors, like Christopher Columbus or Ferdinand Magellan, hail from Wales; but there is Thomas Button of Worleton near Cardiff. He was given a very difficult job. In 1610, the extraordinary explorer, Henry Hudson, had disappeared in Hudson Bay (what a strange coincidence, don't you think?!) in the very north of northern Canada. Thomas Button was sent to find him. But he and his ships were imprisoned by ice in Hudson Bay all through a freezingly cold winter. To keep themselves alive they shot hundreds of white partridges (though not in pear trees!). We don't know whether they found Hudson or not, but two place names – Button Bay and Button Islands – remind us of this story (thanks, Mr Button).

So, Wales isn't famous for its sailors or its explorers, but it is famous for its pirates. Here are the hideous histories of four of those most malicious marauders:

(i) John Callice of Tintern, near Chepstow

Callice captured a Portuguese ship in 1573. The ship was carrying a very valuable cargo of sugar. John sold all the sugar and bought his own ship, the *Olyphant*, with the money. Then, he stole goods from all kinds of ships sailing between Ireland and France.

In fact, Queen Elizabeth I was quite happy for him to steal silver and gold from the ships of the Spanish Catholics!

Before long, however, the plundering pirate had to be caught. One evening he was spotted in Haverfordwest and taken to the Tower of London. But, was John Callice hanged like every other malicious marauder? NO! Somehow he succeeded in getting the Queen's pardon, and he escaped from the Tower a free man!

(ii) Huw Gruffudd from Cefnamlwch, Llŷn

A ship's captain, who became a pillaging pirate. In 1599 he returned home to visit his family and he sailed to Beaumaris to see Sir Richard Bulkeley. But the law was on his tail. His brother, John, galloped all the way from Llŷn to Beaumaris to warn him. Huw sold his expensive cargo; Sir Richard Bulkeley bought the ship himself and Huw disappeared into thin air. (There wasn't much hope of catching a pirate when a Justice of the Peace, like Sir Richard, was willing to help him, was there?)

According to the story, Huw Gruffudd was a very cruel man. He would beat sailors and torture ships' captains to force them to tell him where they had hidden their treasure.

(iii) Tomos Prys of Plasiolyn, Denbighshire

He was quite a character. Tomos wanted to get rich, quick. He bought a ship and began attacking Spanish ships, with the help of his friend Pyrs Gruffudd.

They had such fun that they began to write funny poems to one another describing their amazing adventures. Some of the poems are a mixture of Welsh and English, like this one which describes attacking a ship:

> Shwt *(Shoot) again, broadside,* gynner *(gunner)!*
> *We'll be* braf *(fine) if we* haf *(have) her.*

What would your wise Welsh teachers say if you wrote such doggerel (rubbishy rhymes)?

Tomos Prys spent a lot of his time in London. He claimed to be the first person to smoke tobacco on the city's streets.

Look, that man's head's on fire!

(iv) A Sea Shanty about Henry Morgan, the Boldest Pirate of Them All

Now listen to my stirring tale
How once a boy was forced to sail,
A buccaneer he soon became
And Henry Morgan was his name.

Llanrumney's son was born to be
The boldest pirate on the sea!
From Mexico to Panama
His reputation spread afar.

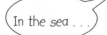

In sixteen sixty-nine he lay
At Maracaibo in the bay
But Spanish ships were lurking near
Intent on blocking his career.

With tar and powder Henry crammed
His ship, and with this 'bomb' he rammed
The 'Magdalena'. What a sight!
To see the enemy's fleet alight.

But Spanish guns kept watch from shore
Determined to redress the score.
They thought that their blockade would thwart
Henry's ships from leaving port.

But Henry had a cunning ruse
To row his men in ones and twos
From ship to shore, first out then back:
An army ready to attack!

The sailors rowed from boat to land
All night and, just as Henry planned,
The Spanish, fearing troops galore
Had landed, turned their guns to shore.

So, with the 'Magdalena's' gold
And Spanish treasure in his hold,
Henry Morgan, safe and sound,
Escaped his foes, Jamaica-bound.

For years to come his ships were caught
But punishment he set at nought
And though he was the worst of cheats,
King Charles admired his roguish feats.

The King enhanced his subject's name
By knighting him. And further fame
Came Henry's way. There's no mistake here:
Charles made him governor of Jamaica.

The story has a bitter close,
As every reader surely knows,
When Henry, much too fond of rum,
Fell ill and died. His end had come!

Goo goo! I come from LlanRUMney.

[Captain Morgan's rum is still popular today and Henry's picture still appears on the bottle!]

Henry Morgan was buried at Port Royal, Jamaica. But in 1692, four years after his death, a huge earthquake shook Port Royal, and the town and Henry Morgan's grave were swept away to the bottom of the sea (quite right – just the place for such a plundering pirate!).

†HE SHAMBOLIC SHIPWRECK

Around the coastline of Wales there are rugged rocks, and in stormy weather sailing ships would be thrown against them and wrecked. Some Welsh people were glad when this happened because they could steal the cargo, have a huge beach party and drink all the brandy and wine.

Once upon a time, two wastefully wealthy families in Glamorgan competed bitterly for this booty from the sea:

SIR GEORGE HERBERT'S FAMILY Sir George was the steward of the Lordship of Gower and Member of Parliament for Glamorgan; he lived in Swansea. He hated Rhys Mansell and his family.	**RHYS MANSELL'S FAMILY** Mansell owned Oxwich and Margam castles. He had his own private little army of 50 men. He hated Herbert and his family.
On 26 December 1557 in the rectory in Oxwich some local gentry, including Mansell, were enjoying a nice Boxing Day dinner. Suddenly the door opened and in came 5 very wet and tired soldiers.	Soldier 1: 'Help! Help! Le ship is on les rocks. Everyone est mort!' The gentry jumped up – French soldiers! – and Britain was at war with France at this time. 'Throw them into prison,' they shouted.
The gentry and all the villagers ran down to the beach to steal the cargo from the shipwreck. They found almonds, raisins, wool and figs. And Rhys Mansell gathered a wagon full of goods to take back to Oxwich Castle.	But George Herbert heard about the shipwreck, and as he was the Sheriff of Glamorgan, he claimed that the cargo and the prisoners were HIS, not Mansell's. He rushed down to Oxwich Castle at once to claim the loot.

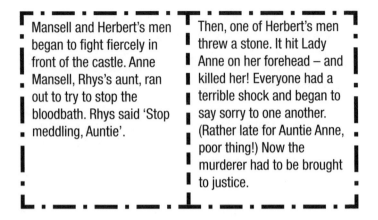

Mansell and Herbert's men began to fight fiercely in front of the castle. Anne Mansell, Rhys's aunt, ran out to try to stop the bloodbath. Rhys said 'Stop meddling, Auntie'.

Then, one of Herbert's men threw a stone. It hit Lady Anne on her forehead – and killed her! Everyone had a terrible shock and began to say sorry to one another. (Rather late for Auntie Anne, poor thing!) Now the murderer had to be brought to justice.

But before the scuffle became a Civil War in Swansea, Elizabeth I was crowned Queen (in 1558) and she decided to pardon everyone involved (good old Queen Bess!).

And that was the end of the story of the shambolic shipwreck.

More Squabbling and Bickering about Religion: Round Two

The Protestants won the first round in the squabbling and bickering about religion. They beat the Catholics. By about 1600 – so they said – there were only 808 Catholics left in the whole of Wales, but maybe there were a few others hiding in holes and caves.

Now the Protestants began to squabble and bicker amongst themselves.

John Penry, the Provocative Protestant

John Penry was never happy. He was a Puritan who wanted to 'purify' the Church of England. He moved from Llangamarch, in Breconshire, to London so that he could complain and criticise the Church properly. He thought the Church was disgraceful:

The bishops are supposed to look after the Church, but they are killing and stifling the spirit of the Welsh people. The priests get drunk, they steal and beg and they are like mute dogs which would rather sleep than help the people. They swear and say stupid things like 'the Devil take my soul'. Wales is a dark and very miserable corner in which to live.

He didn't make many friends penning pamphlets like that! The Church and its Head, the Queen herself, decided he should be hanged – on 29 May 1593. No more penning after that!

Before he was executed (it would have been difficult to manage after he had died!), he wrote a letter to his four little girls – Comfort, Deliverance, Safety and Sure Hope. Unfortunately, their names didn't give their dad much comfort or hope, poor thing!

In fact, very few people in Wales knew about John Penry, the Welsh martyr, because he wrote his leaflets in English and most people couldn't read at all, let alone read English.

The Peevish Puritans

The peevish Puritans were never very popular in Wales. It's hardly surprising, really, because they had some ridiculous rules. Perhaps they just enjoyed spoiling everyone else's fun:

The Peevish Puritans' Five Commandments:

1. Thou shalt not read rubbish (like this book about Wicked Wales) – only the Bible.

2. Thou shalt not play ball on a Sunday (you'll have to go to see Wales playing on a Saturday, then).

3. Thou shalt not swear (Dash! *****).

4. Thou shalt not wear grand garments – only plain, bo-ring clothes.

5. Thou shalt not celebrate Christmas (no Father Christmas, no presents, no Christmas dinner . . .)!

It's not surprising no one liked them, is it? And there were some very sad vicars, like Vicar Prichard of Llandovery, Carmarthenshire, who agreed with the Puritans. He wrote hundreds of vile little verses to tell the Welsh people how to behave and what was good for them:

Better than gold this Bible of mine,
Better than pans or cauldrons fine,
Better than tables or chairs in your hall
Is this little book, most precious of all.

But I can't **cook** with a Bible, Vicar!

As you can see, the old vicar wasn't much of a poet (you could write better verses if you tried), but the Welsh people loved his work and they could recite hundreds of verses from memory:

> *On Sundays do not take your ease*
> *Or drink strong ale or cruelly tease.*
> *The Lord has set this day for you,*
> *And all mankind, his work to do.*

(There you are, then!)

The Quaking Quakers

The sleazy Stuarts thought that the quaking Quakers had the weirdest of weird ideas. They believed that going to war was wrong, and that EVERYONE was equal – as good as one another!!! – a particularly peculiar and incredibly odd idea in the Early Modern Period. Would you like to join them? Well then, you would need to follow these gorgeous guidelines:

The Quakers' Gorgeous Guidelines

1. Don't take your hat off, or bow or curtsey to anyone (especially to your head teacher).
2. Greet everyone in the same way. When speaking Welsh use the familiar 'TI' with everyone and not the polite 'CHI' (just try this with your teachers to see whether they agree!).
3. Remember that men and women are equal (of course).
4. Don't pledge an oath on the Bible.
5. Don't pay the tithe (one tenth of your scarce pocket money) to the Church.
6. Don't set foot inside churches.
7. Don't carry weapons.
8. Don't eat mince pies.

The Quakers even encouraged their women to preach (and some women are very good at preaching!), but many people didn't like this at all. Many Quakers were punished for their incredible ideas. A man called John Humphrey wrote the Quakers' hideous history in his *Great Book of Suffering*. In it he describes how they were treated. These terrible tales come from his book:

1658

The congregation in Llandaff, Cardiff, attacked **Alice Birkett** for trying to speak to the local priest (just imagine – speaking to a priest!). They cut off her clothes and then threw stones at her.

Iechyd da, everyone! Hick!

Elizabeth Holme was thrown into prison in Swansea for interrupting a priest when he was speaking. She was bound by a chain round her leg. Visitors were not allowed to see her or bring her food. All she had to drink was some beer, which she could suck through a straw through the prison bars.

1661

Soldiers interrupted a Quaker meeting in Llwyngwril, Meirionethshire. They gathered the women together and chased them on horseback, making the women run barefoot for twenty miles across the countryside.

I don't like this way of keeping fit – give me a gym any day!

1662

Charles Lloyd of Dolobran, Montgomeryshire, was imprisoned for refusing to attend church! The prison was disgustingly dirty. His wife, Elizabeth, decided to leave their little baby with friends and come to live with Charles in prison. Sewage from the cell above them, where real crooks and criminals were housed, dripped down on top of poor old Charles and Elizabeth Lloyd (*ych-a-fi!*). They spent ten long years in this prison.

That'll teach you a lesson for doing such a dreadfully wicked thing as refusing to attend church!

Have you had enough? Do you want a better world?
Leave all your troubles at home!
Come to live in the Promised Land

NORTH AMERICA

Land and plenty of space for everyone!
Don't miss your chance!

*Contact William Penn
And come to Pennsylvania!*

And that's what Thomas Lloyd of Dolobran (Charles Lloyd's brother), decided to do. He and his wife were tired of being punished and imprisoned for being Quakers. So they packed their bags (pyjamas, teddies and all) and sailed, with their eight children, on a ship bound for Pennsylvania in 1683. Many other Welsh Quakers sailed with them. They wanted to establish a 'Little Wales' out there – to govern themselves, using the Welsh language. They called the area and the villages Meirion, Newtown and Haverford, after place names in Wales. They made friends with the native Indians and Thomas Lloyd became one of Pennsylvania's leaders, when William Penn had to go away.

BUT it all came to a sticky end. By 1693 the English Crown had taken over the state of Pennsylvania and that was the end of the Great Welsh Dream.

The Stuarts in a Stew: The Confusing Civil War

The hideous history of the Civil War is very confusing indeed. Most probably your teachers don't have a CLUE who fought whom, or why. So, here is a CONFUSING QUIZ to help you know more than your terrible teachers.

A Confusing Quiz about the Civil War

1. What was the Civil War (known in Welsh as the '*Rhyfel Cartre*', or '*Home* War')?

    (a) a war in somebody's home, like yours perhaps: brothers against sisters (with the girls winning, of course!).

    (b) a vile video game – 'Civil War' – with two families fighting and killing one another but being very polite or 'civil' about it.

    (c) a fight between King Charles and his friends against the Parliamentarians or Roundheads.

2. When did the Civil War occur?

    (a) All the time. (In your home civil war never stops.)

    (b) Between 1642 and 1649.

    (c) Every Wednesday and Saturday. (Just like football fixtures, but a bit more violent.)

3. Why did they fight a Civil War?

   (a) King Charles I thought God had chosen HIM to be king to rule the country, so everyone should obey him.

   (b) The Parliamentarians said that the people had chosen THEM to rule the country. (Sorry, Charles!)

   (c) The people of Wales had no idea why they were fighting, because no one had explained the reasons to them in Welsh.

4. On whose side were the Welsh people?

Eeny, meeny, miney, may, who shall I support today?

   (a) The Welsh people were fickle and unpredictable – they changed sides as the war went on.

   (b) On the side of the King – because they were quite fond of old Charlie.

   (c) On Parliament's side – especially when Parliament was winning.

5. What kind of soldiers were the Welsh?

   (a) Brilliant – they loved killing and murdering.

   (b) Pathetic – they ran off halfway through a battle.

(c) OK – but they didn't have enough money to buy good weapons.

6. How much fighting took place in Wales itself?

(a) Not much – both the King and the Parliamentarians were much more interested in London than in poor little Wales.

(b) Far too much – the Parliamentarians were hiding under every bed and in every nook and cranny they could find.

(c) Only a few big battles were fought in Wales.

7. What was the outcome of the Civil War?

(a) King Charles I lost his head. Indeed he did!

(b) Parliament began to rule the land.

(c) The Parliamentarians were so hopeless at ruling the country that their leader, Oliver Cromwell, decided to rule the land himself (a kind of mini-king but calling himself 'Lord Protector of the People'). But perhaps the people needed to be protected from Cromwell himself!

4. (a), (b) and (c) are correct here too! – very confusing. On the whole the Welsh sided with the King. Some Welshmen spent a lot of money supporting him. Sir Roger Mostyn claimed that he spent £60,000 on the King's cause. But south Pembrokeshire and the Wrexham area were on Parliament's side. And several Welshmen changed their minds during the War. Sir Hugh Orielton was on Parliament's side until 1644, on the King's side until 1648, and then turned to back Parliament again (what a turncoat!).

5. Unfortunately (b) and (c) are both near the mark. The Welsh soldiers did not have a good reputation. They were called 'poor Taffies' (not Welsh toffees!), because they only had pitchforks and spades as weapons. And when Thomas Dabridgecourt was asked to take charge of the Welsh soldiers, he moaned:

> If your Majesty (the King) put me in charge of the Turks (the people of Turkey not Christmas turkeys) or the Jews or anyone else, I would be willing to go barefoot to please you, but please (please, please) don't send me to Wales to be in charge of the Welsh!

The prickly pamphlets of the pompous Parliamentarians said some disgraceful things about the Welsh. They said they were 'wicked, spiteful people – worse than barbarians!' (How wicked is that!)

6. (c) Some important battles, including the famous Battle of St Fagans (NOT in the National History Museum!), on 8 May 1648, were fought in Wales. Rather oddly, the Second Civil War was started by Parliamentarians from south Pembrokeshire.

The leaders were Rice Powell, Rowland Laugharne and John Poyer. Suddenly, they decided to change sides to support the King, and fight against their old friends, the Parliamentarians. They lost the battle and the three leaders were caught and sentenced to death. But they decided to hold a raffle to choose ONE of them to die on behalf of the other two. Poor old Poyer – HE won the raffle and he was shot dead by a firing squad at Covent Garden, London. Out of the three rebels' followers, 240 were punished by being transported to live in the sun in Barbados. (A punishment?)

7. (a), (b) and (c) – Charles lost his head on 30 January, 1649. According to one Welshman, who watched the execution, he heard: 'a great sigh coming from the thousands present. I never heard anything like it before and I wouldn't like to hear anything like it ever again!'

Sensational Stars

During the troublesome Tudor and sleazy Stuart ages the Welsh were full of confidence and one or two became sensational stars in wicked Wales, England and the world.

Test your history teachers to see whether they have heard of these very important men – and use stars to score them.

Robert Recorde (1510–1558)

From Tenby. Recorde wrote the first mathematics book in English (a very black star for that), and he invented the symbol = to show when things are equal. He became head of the Royal Mint (where money is made, not sweets!) and he was physician to Edward VI and Mary Tudor (but Edward died when he was just sixteen years old and Mary when she was forty-two – what a good doctor!). Recorde died in prison in London. (Serve him right for trying to torture Welsh children with his maths.)

Number of stars = ★★★

Thomas Jenkins *(no idea when or where he was born, or when he died)*

He taught the most important playwright in the world – William Shakespeare (1564–1616). Shakespeare learnt everything from this Welshman at Stratford-upon-Avon's Grammar School. They say that Shakespeare had Thomas Jenkins in mind when he wrote the part of Sir Hugh Evans in his comedy, *The Merry Wives of Windsor*. In the play, Sir Hugh Evans speaks English just as Shakespeare imagined Welsh people spoke it – saying things like 'fery goot' for 'very good'; 'petter' for 'better'; and 'ork' for 'work'.
Number of stars = ★★★★★

Unknown

They say that a Welshman living during the Elizabethan Age was the first to invent a language for people who were deaf and dumb – and in the Welsh language at that. (What a pity that language was lost, isn't it?)
Number of stars = ★★★★★ – if your teachers have ever heard of this!

John Dee (1527–1608)

Though he was born in London, his family came from Powys. John Dee was a mathematician, but he was also an astrologer who loved studying the stars. Queen Elizabeth 1 doted on him. She asked him to prove that she was the owner of the new lands in North America. As a Welshman, John Dee knew the story of Prince Madog, who had, according to legend, sailed to America in 1170. Since Elizabeth could claim some Welsh blood (a tiny, tiny drop), she said she was related to Prince Madog. So, there wasn't a problem, was there? (Only for the Spaniards who also claimed the land, and the native Indians who already lived there!) Some said that Dee used a crystal ball to talk to evil spirits.

Number of stars = ★★★

Sir Hugh Myddleton (1560–1631)

He came from Denbigh. He made a great deal of money through his gold and silver businesses. He went to live in London. But about 180,000 other people also lived in London and there was no sewage system (to carry the toilet waste away), and no fresh water for people to drink there. The river Thames was full of filth, rubbish and dead animals: the city was very unhealthy and stank to high heaven. Hugh Myddleton decided to bring clean water to London with his 'New River Project'. He spent £2,000 a month on this project. Rather spitefully, the Welshman Sir John Wynne said about this venture, 'What a pity he didn't spend some of the money in his own country.' (Fair point, perhaps!)

Number of stars = ★★★

EDWARD LHUYD (1660–1709)

His parents were Welsh, but he lived over the border in England. When he was working at Oxford University he began to take an interest in the Celtic countries and to collect information about Celtic languages (Welsh, Irish, Gaelic . . .).

He wrote a huge (and rather boring) book called *Archaeologia Britannica*. He liked the world of nature and plants. (What a pity he spelt his own name so strangely, though!)
Number of stars = ★★★

How many of these sensational stars are familiar to your history teachers? How many stars have they won?

Unfortunately there were some Welshmen who had a talent for being stupid too:

WILLIAM VAUGHAN FROM GOLDEN GROVE, CARMARTHENSHIRE (1575–1641)

Because he was sad to see so many pitifully poor Welsh people, Vaughan bought land in Newfoundland in the very far north of North America. He called this new country 'Cambriol' (like *Cambria* or *Cymru* – Wales). He didn't go out there himself (he was too wise to fall into that trap). The country was so cold and miserable the poor old Welsh nearly starved to death. Within twelve years this strange experiment had failed completely and many of them had returned to live in poor Wales. Give him a black mark ● for being so stupid, and two black marks ●● each to the Welsh people who believed in his stupid plan.